THE

CirclePoint
METHOD

Practical and Integrated Mechanisms for
PREVENTING and **RESOLVING**
Bullying Issues in Schools

ARI MAGNUSSON

OLIVANDER PRESS LLC
Winchester, Massachusetts, USA

Olivander, Olivander Press, CirclePoint Bullying Prevention Resources, CirclePoint Method, and associated logos are trademarks of Olivander Press LLC.

Paperback ISBN-13: 979-8-9897557-0-7
eBook ISBN-13: 979-8-9897557-1-4

First edition, February 2024

Printed in the United States of America
Cover and interior design by Liz Schreiter

To Michele Davis, for setting such a high bar
and then working tirelessly to raise it

About This Guide

The CirclePoint Method is a comprehensive set of integrated mechanisms that were tested in a K–8 school in the Boston Public School District in the state of Massachusetts, USA, in 2016 and found to be highly effective at preventing and resolving bullying issues. The mechanisms were relatively easy to implement and saved educators significant time compared to using traditional practices. More importantly, the sustained use of these mechanisms created a school environment where bullying behaviors became less accepted by students over time, allowing students to feel safe and accepted and to focus on learning.

This guide describes the mechanisms in detail and provides suggestions for implementation. The mechanisms are based on a modern understanding of bullying and were designed to supplant traditional bullying prevention policies and approaches while allowing educators to maintain compliance with typical district reporting and discipline requirements. Please note that this guide is not intended to help educators address all aggressive behavior in students, particularly behavior driven by mental health issues where intervention by counselors or mental health professionals is required.

The information in this guide is primarily intended for administrators, teachers, and support staff in elementary and middle schools and their equivalents outside of the United States. The Method can also be used by any organization where adults work with young people, such as after-school programs and youth camps.

In order to describe the mechanisms as simply as possible, the text does not burden readers with references or footnotes for all of the supporting research. However, a comprehensive bibliography is included at the end of the guide. In addition, appendices provide supporting information and deeper dives into select topics. Further, the CirclePoint website (circlepointbullying.com) provides updates and addenda to this guide.

Why Bullying Prevention and Issue Resolution Are Critical

A safe environment where students feel accepted by peers is the foundation for a good education. Students being harmed by aggression are not able to focus on learning. Educators should make bullying prevention a top priority for many reasons, including the following:

- Bullying causes harm. Unlike physical assault, however, the harm caused by bullying is not always visible. And while the wounds caused by a physical assault may heal quickly, the harm caused by bullying can last a lifetime. Just because the harm cannot be seen, it doesn't mean it is not occurring. Educators should not differentiate between visible harm and invisible harm in terms of their efforts to prevent and stop it.

- Students who are being bullied by a peer and who are forced to be with that peer are essentially trapped in an abusive relationship. The adults who manage the environment in which this abuse is occurring have a moral and ethical responsibility to identify it, stop it, and prevent further instances of it.

- Bullied students cannot focus on their schoolwork, which is why a decline in grades is often cited as a sign of a child being bullied. Given the numbers of students who are being bullied in a school at any one time (20–30%, depending upon the research study), addressing the bullying problems in a school should result in better overall test scores for the student body.

- Bullying can lead to tragic outcomes, and schools can be held accountable (multimillion-dollar settlements are becoming the norm). From a liability risk mitigation perspective, schools need to do all they can to implement effective mechanisms to ensure that these tragedies do not happen.

A Note on Terminology

This guide uses the following terms:

- **school:** an organization using the Method
- **principal:** head administrator of the organization
- **educators:** a collective term for the adults who work in a school that includes the principal or head of school, administrators, teachers, monitors, counselors, psychologists, and other staff
- **parent:** the functional role of one or more adults with primary responsibility for a student outside of school; the adult(s) can be biologically related to or legal caretakers of the student and can include a parent, stepparent, grandparent, other family member, or guardian
- **mechanism:** one or more actions, processes, or strategies designed to achieve a specific outcome related to bullying prevention and problem resolution

A Note on Pronouns

For simplicity, this guide uses one set of consistent pronouns when explaining a topic. For example, a topic might use the pronouns "he" to refer to an aggressor and "she" to refer to a principal when describing a hypothetical bullying scenario. Unless explicitly stated, the use of pronouns is not meant to associate a specific gender identity with certain behaviors or imply that a specific type of bullying is limited to a particular gender. Pronouns have been selected for readability and to avoid using a multipronoun construct (i.e., "he/she/ze/they") in the text. The pronouns "he" and "she" are used in this guide since nonbinary pronouns are still evolving in the English language. The lack of nonbinary pronouns is not meant to minimize or indicate rejection of their importance or the general need for inclusive language.

Contents

Introduction
Method Overview

The CirclePoint Method consists of the following mechanisms:

Key Terms and Language (Chapter 1)

The language used when discussing bullying can affect outcomes. Some traditional bullying-related terms are subjective and carry negative connotations, the use of which can make successful resolution of issues more difficult. Having everyone use a common language of objective terms avoids these negative connotations, leading to easier resolution.

Staff Education (Chapters 2 and 3)

Education on bullying for all stakeholders—educators, students, and parents—is critical to successfully preventing and resolving bullying issues. In order to be applied effectively, the integrated mechanisms of the Method require an accurate understanding of bullying, free from the myths and misconceptions that traditionally characterize the topic. Education for staff is described in two chapters due to the complexity of the topic. Education for students is described in chapter 10. Education for parents is described in chapter 11.

Constructive Consequences (Chapter 4)

Constructive Consequences is a way of resolving bullying problems by leveraging the same drivers of aggression to get it to stop. The mechanism involves having a discussion with an aggressor to make him aware that he is causing harm; giving him an opportunity to stop in order to avoid a consequence; letting him know that the adults who are with him and the target will be watching to ensure the behavior stops; and applying a consequence if the aggression continues. The consequence consists of a separation from peers during the times when the aggression against the target has occurred. The aggressor will perceive the separation as having a negative effect on social status, which will motivate the aggressor to change his behavior toward the target.

Chain of Custody Awareness (Chapter 5)

Chain of Custody Awareness is the communication of a bullying issue to all adults who are with a target during the school day and, optionally, at home, in order to monitor the behavior of the aggressor toward the target to ensure bullying has stopped. Any instances of aggression are documented and reported. The heightened monitoring ends when the bullying issue is confirmed to be resolved, usually after a few days. Both the aggressor and target are aware that adults are monitoring them so that the aggressor has an incentive to stop the behavior and the target feels safe. The mechanism is used in tandem with Constructive Consequences.

Target Support—The Five-Step Framework (Chapter 6)

Target Support consists of the Five-Step Framework, a discussion outline used to guide support conversations with targets. The framework is designed to help the target heal, educate the target on bullying, and empower the target to take effective action to get the bullying to stop. The framework is informal, meaning that discussions that do not cover all five steps can still be helpful to the target. The number of steps used in the discussion will depend on target need and the circumstances of the bullying issue.

Removal of Barriers to Reporting (Chapter 7)

Barriers to reporting prevent targets from coming forward to seek help with a bullying problem. The Removal of Barriers to Reporting mechanism is a collection of steps that schools can take to eliminate these barriers so bullied students will proactively self-identify and students aware of bullying issues involving peers will notify educators. This mechanism should help surface bullying issues early, before targets suffer significant harm and when issues can be most easily resolved, and ensures that educators are aware of most, if not all, of the bullying issues occurring at any one time.

Antibullying Announcement (Chapter 8)

The Antibullying Announcement is a periodic announcement about bullying that lets students know that adults do not condone bullying behaviors, makes students aware that adults need help in identifying bullying problems, and explains how adults will handle bullying problems when students come forward. This mechanism helps remove a barrier to reporting by providing students with assurances that asking adults for help will not make the problem worse. Periodic delivery is needed to reach those students who are newly involved in a bullying issue.

Classroom Strategies (Chapter 9)

Educators who are with the same group of students on a regular basis (e.g., classroom teachers) occupy a unique position as they know best their students' social structures and interpersonal dynamics. These educators can use a variety of proactive and reactive Classroom Strategies to influence individual students and groups of students to positively change the culture around aggression; identify those suffering harm and intervene; and provide support to targets.

Student Education and Empowerment (Chapter 10)

Student Education and Empowerment is critical to success. Students who understand what bullying is, why peers do it, and what they can do to get it to stop can avoid the harm caused by aggression and resolve issues on their own. This mechanism includes bystander activation and empowerment so that students learn low-risk and risk-free ways of helping bullied peers without the risk of becoming targets themselves.

Parent Education and Engagement (Chapter 11)

Parents need to work in partnership with their children and educators on resolving bullying problems. Parent Education and Engagement is important as it ensures that parents' understanding of bullying is accurate and aligned with educators. The CirclePoint website (www.circlepointbullying.com) provides the parent education component. Due to differences in the understanding of bullying that parents invariably have, educators need to take care in how they engage with parents and the language they use when trying to resolve a bullying issue.

Implementation (Chapter 12)

The Method can be implemented in a variety of ways, depending on time and resources. However, four phases are recommended. Schools need to: 1. prepare for implementation by developing a plan and gathering materials; 2. educate staff on bullying and the Method's mechanisms; 3. practice the mechanisms in order to reach a level of proficiency that ensures that student trust will be maintained; and 4. initiate student and parent engagement.

Key Terms and Language

1

Overview: The terms and language used in resolving a bullying issue can affect the outcome. Some traditional bullying terms, such as "bully" and "victim," carry negative connotations that can impede resolution. Even the term "bullying" is problematic. Using objective terminology and being sensitive to how certain terms are perceived help avoid negative responses and ensure an accurate understanding of the issue by all stakeholders—educators, students, and parents.

Key Terms

The following terms are problematic:

- **bully:** a term that is a label and is dehumanizing. In addition, the term carries negative connotations about the person's character. A person might use bullying behavior in their interactions; however, no person is a "bully." The term should never be used to describe an individual.
- **victim:** a term that carries negative connotations of helplessness and an inability to respond or take action. The term should be avoided.

The following terms are recommended:

- **aggression:** a broad and general term that describes a wide variety of behaviors, including pushing, shoving, teasing, mocking, intimidating, antagonizing, and socially excluding. Aggression is delivered face-to-face; indirectly, such as through rumors; and in writing, such as on paper or objects, or virtually through social media. Aggression is both normal and common in student social interactions, including between good friends. The majority of aggression is not harmful.
- **aggressor:** the person in a social interaction who directs aggression at another person, and in cases where multiple individuals are using aggression, the person(s) who initiates or leads the aggression. The use of the term does not imply any sort of judgment about the person or action.

- **target:** the person in a social interaction at whom aggression is directed. For simplicity, this guide uses the term "target" to indicate both those who are harmed and not harmed by the aggression. A more accurate term for the person who is harmed is "affected target." When the term "target" is used in this guide, the context is always provided to indicate the meaning, i.e., whether the target is harmed or not.
- **supporter:** a person who follows an aggressor's lead and also directs aggression at the target.
- **bystander:** a person who is witness to aggression. The bystander can be "active" in that he shows explicit approval of the aggressor's behavior through either physical or verbal actions or body language, or a bystander can be "passive" in that he observes aggression but does not indicate support for the aggressor.
- **participant:** a person who supports the efforts of an aggressor to socially isolate a target. This term is specific to relational aggression, which is described in chapter 2.
- **chronic target:** a person who has consistently been a target of peers for a period of time such that the use of aggression toward that person is viewed as normal and natural behavior by members of the peer group.

Use of the Term "Bullying"

The term "bullying" presents challenges in that its use and meaning can vary based on the knowledge and perspective of the stakeholder. Its use in certain contexts can make resolving an issue more difficult and trigger required but sometimes counterproductive actions based on district requirements and state laws. Consider the following:

- An aggressor who is unaware that his behavior is causing harm will not understand why such a negative and derogatory the term is being used. Using the term "bullying" to describe behavior that the aggressor considers to be innocuous can make the aggressor feel unjustly accused of an inappropriate action. This notion is described in chapter 2.
- Given the negative connotations of the term with respect to the aggressor's character or intent, use of the term can elicit strong negative reactions from the aggressor's parents, who may also feel that their child is being falsely or unjustly accused. Parents who are told their child is "bullying another" may become defensive and antagonistic toward educators and want to shield their child from these "accusations." Some parents may become angry with their child, mistakenly understanding "bullying" to mean intentional harm. Parents of the target who are told that their child is "being bullied" will want to protect their child. They may blame the school for the problem and demand justice. In addition, the term "bullying" can have different meanings in different cultures. To some parents of certain ethnicities, the term can be a significant indictment of the child, whether the child is the aggressor or the target.

- Students, particularly younger ones, use the term to complain about aggression that is not causing harm but rather is bothersome or annoying. Educators need to take care in its use to ensure students do not apply it to instances of less serious aggression.
- Society has been conditioned to think of bullying very negatively and that the consequence for such a negative, harmful action should be punitive. This negative response and automatic association with punishment is counterproductive.
- Use of the term in certain administrative contexts can trigger reporting requirements and punitive actions that are often unnecessary and counterproductive.

Suggested Conversation Guidelines

The way bullying issues are discussed and the terms that are used should vary based on the stakeholder and context:

- In general, use language that describes behaviors, responses, and feelings instead of using formal terms. The statement "Student A has been constantly mocking Student B, which has made Student B feel rejected by classmates and flawed" means the same as "Student A was the aggressor who directed verbal aggression at the target, Student B, resulting in bullying" but avoids the formal terms.
- Educators discussing issues among themselves can certainly use the recommended key terms above to ensure consistent and clear communication. Educators should be careful, however, not to overuse the term "bullying." When harm to a target has been confirmed, the term can be used. Where harm is suspected, a description of the behavior should be used.
- When talking with students, educators should use the term "bullying" generally (e.g., the school is trying to prevent bullying, teachers do not condone bullying). Limiting use to general contexts avoids diluting the meaning and impact of the word through overuse and avoids having students adopt the word as a synonym for being bothered or annoyed by another student. In cases where an aggressor is causing harm but may not be aware of it, educators should simply describe the behavior and the effect on the target. Only when an aggressor is aware of the harm that results from the aggression and continues the aggression should the term "bullying" be used.
- In conversations with parents, educators should describe the aggressor's behavior as well as the target's responses and feelings, and refer to the students by name. Even the recommended terms of "aggressor" and "target" can elicit strong negative reactions and make problem resolution difficult. Detailed guidelines for conversations with parents are provided in chapter 11.

- Educators should be aware of their district's official, published definition of bullying, which may be a traditional definition that differs from the one in this Method. Awareness of the district definition is important so that educators can avoid using the term "bullying" in contexts that will trigger reporting requirements or a counterproductive disciplinary action. More information on the problems with traditional bullying definitions and why they should not be used as the basis for bullying prevention policies and procedures is provided in appendix A.

Staff Education
Fundamentals

2

Overview: The key to understanding bullying is to start not with a definition but rather with the drivers of student behavior and the effect this behavior can have on peers. Once these are understood, the definition of bullying becomes clear, as do the rationales behind the Method's mechanisms. This understanding will make it easier for staff to reject outdated and inaccurate ideas about bullying based on flawed information, preconceived notions due to negative personal experiences, and misguided perceptions of observed behavior.

Social Status: The Driver of Student Behavior

Student behavior is driven by the primary goal of improving social standing among peers. In general, except for what is required by others (such as teachers and parents), everything students do is influenced, if not fully driven, by an all-consuming need for peer approval. Social status becomes the number one priority for girls starting around kindergarten and for boys at around third grade, with nonbinary students likely falling somewhere within that range. When students interact with each other, they are not thinking so much about how their behavior affects others but rather how their behavior benefits their own social status.

Social status is so important to students that the majority (75%) will break a school rule if doing so improves their status. For example, if a teacher tells all students to be quiet but a student thinks of a comment that will make peers laugh, the student will likely make the comment despite the teacher's directive for silence. Students will generally do everything they can to be accepted by their peers and gain their approval. Further, the need to maintain status is what drives students to want to stay constantly connected with peers, either in person or virtually. Just as importantly, students will do all they can to avoid behaviors that would make them look bad in the eyes of their peers.

Peer Approval Requires a Peer Audience

All student behavior that is intended to have a positive effect on social status, i.e., maintain or increase status, occurs in front of a peer audience because peers determine an individual's status through approval and validation. The student who makes a funny comment to his friends after being told not to talk believes the benefit provided by cracking a joke in front of his peer audience outweighs the consequence, such as a reprimand. If that student did not have that peer audience—if he were sitting alone or not near friends—he would not have the same incentive to speak.

Students will do or say things considered outlandish or shocking, such as vandalism or saying something terrible to a peer, in front of a peer audience if they believe the increase in social status outweighs the consequence. When presented with an opportunity to improve status, some students will not even consider the consequences of their behavior.

Student behavior can change significantly when the peer audience is not present. A student who constantly teases another student in front of others in order to get peers to laugh may not tease that student when the two of them are alone since the sole purpose of the teasing is peer approval.

Favorite and Most Dreaded Time of the School Day

Many students' favorite time of the school day is any time when they can freely interact with their peers. Unrestricted or lightly monitored social time is when students are able to work on their social status. Those times generally include time between classes, recess, and lunch, which are when direct student aggression most frequently occurs. In schools that do not restrict social media access during the school day, that time to freely interact with peers can be all day long.

Unrestricted social time is also the time dreaded by students who are the targets of unwanted aggression. Some students so dislike this time that they seek ways to avoid it, such as eating lunch in an educator's office or volunteering to "help" an educator during recess. However, in schools that do not restrict social media access, these students may not be able to escape the aggression.

How Aggression Is Used to Positively Affect Social Status

Student interactions involve a constant stream of aggression—pushes, shoves, taunts, mockery, insults, antagonism, social alliances, and exclusion. This aggression can be delivered face-to-face; indirectly (e.g., via rumors); and in writing, both physically, such as on tangible objects like paper or a bathroom stall wall, or virtually, such as through words and images on social media.

Aggression is used to establish social hierarchies within larger groups of students, such as classes. Students in a class use a variety of behaviors to define the social "pecking order." For example, when students move from elementary to middle school and class compositions are maintained from one school to the next, there is generally no change in the level of aggression within the classes as social hierarchies are preserved. But when students move to different schools and class compositions change—students are mixed into different classes—levels of aggression temporarily increase as students reestablish social hierarchies within each class.

Aggression is also used at a smaller group level, such as within a group of friends, to define or assert the group's identity by directing aggression at nonmembers, particularly those who have characteristics or identities different from the group members. A group of students on a sports team may direct aggression at nonteam members. A group of students of a particular ethnicity may direct aggression at others of a different ethnicity. A group of friends may use aggression to let others know that they are not part of the group. It is important to note that this aggression has an inward focus, meaning it serves to reinforce the personal bonds of those in the group, not so much to indicate exclusion or rejection of those outside the group.

Aggression is used at the individual level to positively affect social status. Physical aggression is used to gain respect through intimidation. Teasing, taunts, and mocking, whether in written or verbal form, are used to appear clever or funny to others. Exclusion is used to diminish the social status of another, which can help the person doing the excluding to maintain status. The leader of a group may use aggression against other group members in order to defend the leadership position. Aggression is also directed by an individual in a group at those outside of the group to get affirmation by the other group members that the individual is included in the group.

Aggression between students is normal and natural. The majority of it is not harmful, and students need to learn both how to use it appropriately and how to respond to it effectively in order to develop well-rounded social skills. Students should be free to engage in aggression, even at the risk of some students experiencing discomfort (though not harm), as this provides an opportunity to mature and develop confidence, self-reliance, resilience, and empathy.

Use of Characteristics in Aggression

Some forms of aggression explicitly reference a unique characteristic of the target. This characteristic can be something about the target's appearance, body shape, clothing, family and/ or background, ethnicity, religion, interests, special ability or disability, gender identity, sexual orientation, socioeconomic circumstances, the fact that he is new at school, or any other aspect of the target. In aggression involving groups, characteristics are used to affirm the group's identity (i.e., the group members do not have the characteristic of the target). The selection of a particular characteristic can also reflect prejudice or contempt on the part of the aggressor, such as when the referenced characteristic pertains to ethnicity or involves a stereotype.

Popular Students Determine Accepted Peer Group Behavior

The degree to which behaviors are accepted within a peer group is often determined by the most popular student or students in that peer group. If the most popular student disapproves of how a student is being treated by the peer group, those behaviors may stop. But if a popular student shows approval of or neutrality toward a behavior, the behavior will continue. This influence correlates to how strongly members of the group seek the popular student's approval. If a peer does not care about getting the approval of the most popular student, the popular student's influence on that peer will be limited.

Aggression "Flows" Down Social Structures

Although all students use aggression, it tends to be directed down the social hierarchy within a large peer group such as a class because aggression directed at a peer with a lower social status does not carry the risk of social status loss. A student who directs aggression at a more popular student may find that the peer audience will rally to the side of and support the more popular student since that student's approval is more valuable socially than the aggressor's.

When a student directs aggression at a student with lower status, some peer witnesses may join in (supporters) and direct aggression at the target in an effort to gain the approval of the aggressor and improve their own social status. Other peer witnesses may show implicit support for the aggressor (active bystanders) through reactions (e.g., laughter) or their body language, but not join in and direct aggression at the target. Some bystanders simply observe but don't intervene or show support (passive bystanders). Intervention would mean taking the side of a lower-status student (the target) against not only the higher-status aggressor but also any supporters and active bystanders, which can carry a significant social cost and the risk of becoming a target of the aggression.

In almost all large social groups, such as a class, there are one or two individuals at the bottom of the hierarchy who are targets of aggression by members of the entire group (chronic targets). These individuals have no peer support and are "risk-free" targets since no peers will intervene.

New students are often the target of aggression because they enter a class of students without any peer support and are generally at the bottom of the social structure until they establish friendships. Their position in the social hierarchy will generally be equal to that of their friends. The development of a social network by the new student can be helped or hindered by how the most popular students in the peer group behave toward the new student.

Effect of the Target's Reaction on the Benefits of Aggression

Aggression can positively affect status no matter how the target of the aggression reacts, whether the target laughs, gets angry or upset, shrugs it off, or returns the aggression. Certain reactions can, however, increase the social benefit. A target who exhibits fear from physical aggression delivers on the aggressor's goal of getting a display of deference and respect, which can make observing peers also show respect to the aggressor. A target of verbal aggression who gets upset may increase the social benefit realized by the aggressor as the observing peers may be even more entertained. A target who pretends that aggression intended to socially isolate her is not happening, i.e., the target stands by passively and does not defend herself and her friendships, increases the chance that the aggression will succeed. In all cases of physical and verbal aggression, a reaction by the target that increases the benefit provided by the aggression increases the likelihood that the aggression will be repeated.

Certain reactions by targets can, however, reduce or eliminate the benefits to social status that aggression provides. A target who does not show fear when faced with physical aggression deprives the aggressor of his goal and may even make the aggressor appear foolish to observing peers. A target who laughs along with others at insults or mockery does not make the aggressor appear to be as funny or clever to observing peers and deprives the peer audience of any entertainment that getting upset provides. A target who takes action to defend against an aggressor who is trying to hurt her relationships with friends may cause the aggressor to fail in her efforts. In all of these instances, the target's reaction may actually result in a loss of status by the aggressor, which ensures that the aggression won't be repeated.

Relevance of the Target's Feelings to the Benefits of Aggression

In general, the target's feelings about the aggression are not a factor in the social benefits gained by the aggressor. Except in cases where a target is upset to a degree that goes beyond what peers find acceptable and evokes feelings of pity or empathy toward the target, the way the aggression makes the target feel does not change the benefits. In addition, targets who are harmed by aggression tend to hide or suppress their emotions. Getting emotional in front of peers usually reduces social status. This lack of expression of any hurt caused by the aggression means that aggressors are generally unaware that the target's feelings are hurt. Even when aggressors do become aware of the harm to a target and even feel genuine empathy for the target, so strong is the need for peer approval and so important is social status that aggressors may continue the aggression.

Effect of Aggression on Targets

In many cases, aggression has no significant effect on targets. However, in some cases, aggression causes targets to feel rejected by both the aggressor and any peer witnesses. The actions of supporters and active bystanders are interpreted by the target to be explicit rejection while the passivity of those who observe but don't intervene may be considered implicit rejection. The lack of intervention or support by any peers can make a target feel isolated and alone.

In addition to peer rejection and low social status, aggression can have other negative effects. Physical aggression makes a target feel afraid for his personal safety. Verbal and written aggression explicitly mentioning a characteristic of the target can make the target feel flawed, i.e., that the reason for the peer rejection is due to the characteristic. This type of harm is particularly damaging since a target who feels flawed due to a personal characteristic that cannot be changed may feel that there is nothing that can be done to gain peer approval.

The number of chronic targets in a peer group such as a class is a factor in the harm caused by aggression. One student in a class who is at the bottom of the social hierarchy and who is the sole target of the group's aggression may blame himself for the aggression. Multiple students in a class who are the targets of the group's aggression may blame the aggressors and feel a social connection to each other.

The Definition of Bullying

The modern definition of bullying is as follows:

> **Bullying occurs when aggression causes emotional harm. More specifically, bullying occurs when the use of behaviors intended to positively affect (maintain, increase, or protect) social status among peers causes emotional harm to the target of the behaviors.**

It's important to note that positively affecting one's own social status can include behaviors that diminish the social status of another person.

Three erroneous notions often found in traditional definitions of bullying are important to address here in order to ensure that the modern definition is clearly understood:

1. **intent to harm:** traditional definitions of bullying often include the condition that the aggressor "intends harm." This is generally false. The aggressor intends to positively affect his own social status without regard for how the aggression affects the target. Even when informed that the aggression is causing harm, the aggressor may consider the resulting status benefit to be more important than stopping any harm that is affecting the target. An aggressor who insults a target and elicits a response of laughter from the peer audience is after that peer

response; the aggressor is not thinking about how the target feels. The harm caused by the insult is simply a by-product of the aggressor's desire for that positive peer response. Harm certainly occurs in bullying; however, causing harm to the target is not the primary intent of the aggression. An aggressor can direct identical behaviors at multiple individuals, including close friends. In all instances, the aggressor is seeking a status improvement. Please note that instances of aggression where physical harm occurs is considered assault, not bullying.

2. **repetition:** traditional definitions often require aggression to be "repeated" in order for bullying to be occurring. Repetition falls into a gray area. The behavior will be repeated if it provides a benefit. The repetition occurs because the aggression successfully provides that benefit. But repetition is not necessary for harm to occur. A target who is mocked one time by multiple individuals may experience the same emotional harm as a target mocked multiple times by one person. Aggression done once by multiple individuals to a single target meets the definition of bullying. Students who are chronically bullied and suffering harm may be the target of aggression from an entire class of peers, whose aggression toward that target on an individual basis may be so sporadic or intermittent that to an observing adult the behavior does not appear to fit the definition of "repeated." The aggression that results in social isolation, which is a type of bullying that can cause extreme harm, generally does not involve repeated behaviors.

3. **power imbalance:** traditional definitions try to explain the nature of the social hierarchy and the ability of higher-status students to direct aggression at lower-status students without intervention from peers as a "power imbalance." Some definitions even include a list of "powers," such as physical strength, that are out of balance. The notion of a "power imbalance" is a clumsy and confusing way to explain that in bullying, the aggressor usually has a higher social status than the target. The aggressor has the approval of peers, meaning that no one will side with or come to the defense of the lower-status target due to the risk of losing social status or of becoming a target.

These three notions found in traditional bullying definitions contribute to the erroneous tendency of educators to focus on the aggression instead of the effects on the target to determine whether bullying is occurring. As discussed below, there is a much simpler and accurate way to determine if bullying is occurring. For more information on the problems with the traditional definitions of bullying, see appendix A.

What Makes Aggression Bullying

Aggression can be classified as bullying when the aggression results in harm, specifically a feeling of social rejection by peers. Bullying cannot be determined based on the behavior of the aggressor. An aggressor may direct identical behaviors at multiple individuals, but not every individual is going to be harmed by the behavior.

Types of Aggression Used in Bullying

The aggression involved in bullying can be classified into three different types that reflect the aggressor's intent in terms of the social benefit gained. The behaviors used in each type of aggression, however, can be similar. The following are the three types of aggression:

- **dominance aggression:** a type of aggression where behaviors such as light physical contact; a demeanor projecting fearlessness, anger, or strength; and threats of harm are intended to intimidate a target by instilling a sense of fear of personal harm so that the target and observing peers will respect the aggressor.
- **rejective aggression:** a type of aggression that uses a characteristic of a target to differentiate the target from peers. The characteristic can be related to anything about the target, real or perceived, and can include, but is not limited to, the target's body size and physical features; personality traits; cultural background; ethnicity; socioeconomic standing; a material possession; a talent or skill; achievements and accomplishments; and group affiliation such a sports team, school, or interest group. This type of aggression is used to reinforce the bonds of a peer group, reaffirm membership in a peer group, gain the approval of higher-status peers, and/or diminish a positive aspect of the target.
- **relational aggression:** a type of aggression that is intended to harm the friendships of the target so that the target is left socially isolated. This type of aggression is often used by an aggressor to maintain or protect social status by diminishing the status of the target.

Please note that all three types of aggression are used to create and maintain the social hierarchy of the peer group. Further, some aggressive behaviors may have characteristics of more than one type of aggression, and multiple types of aggression can be used in individual bullying cases. For example, a student may mock a characteristic of another (rejective aggression) in an intimidating manner (dominance aggression) for which the lack of response by the target is meant to show observing peers that the target is afraid of and won't stand up to the aggressor. Or an aggressor may use a trait of a target (rejective aggression) as justification for members of the peer group to shun the target (relational aggression).

Behaviors Common to Each Type of Aggression

Aggression that can instill feelings of peer rejection spans a wide spectrum of behaviors but can generally be classified into the following categories:

- **physical:** often used in dominance aggression, includes actions such as intimidation, light physical contact such as pushes and shoves, and glares to instill fear in a target and respect for the aggressor. Aggressors who engage in physical aggression generally do not intend physical harm.
- **verbal:** used in all three types of aggression, includes face-to-face actions such as mocking, insults, put-downs, and antagonism used in rejective aggression; threats of physical harm typical to dominance aggression; and rumors and other indirect/secretive communications often used in relational aggression.
- **written/expressive:** applicable to all three types of aggression, includes words and images, such as pictures and videos, on paper, on objects, or on social media.
- **exclusion:** applicable to relational aggression, includes actions that are generally indirect, secretive, and nonconfrontational in which peers of a target are asked, influenced, or pressured into severing their friendship with the target. Exclusion behaviors often include direct communications to the target that express or show that the target is no longer a member of the peer group. Exclusion in the context of bullying generally takes the form of a "campaign" in which the aggressor recruits members of the target's peer group to ignore, avoid, or distance themselves from the target and to explicitly communicate to the target that the target is no longer a member of the peer group. Please note that there is a difference between not including a person in an activity or in a peer group and an organized campaign of exclusion initiated by an individual to intentionally get members of the target's peer group to stop being friends with the target. Not including a peer who is not part of a group of friends at the lunch table, in a group activity, or in a social event is not relational aggression (though it may be rejective aggression).

The Emotional Harm Caused by Aggression

The emotional harm caused by aggression involves feelings of peer rejection and diminished self-esteem. However, these feelings can be accompanied by other forms of emotional harm depending upon the type of aggression used:

- Dominance aggression can cause fear of and anxiety about being physically harmed.
- Rejective aggression can cause a sense of being flawed due to a personal characteristic.
- Relational aggression can cause feelings of social isolation and abandonment by friends.

These different types of harm are important to understand in order to ensure that targets receive appropriate support.

Cyberbullying

Despite having "bullying" in its name, cyberbullying is not a type of bullying. Cyberbullying is the use of social media to direct aggression at a target. A text from an aggressor to a target saying "see you in gym class" when gym class is where the aggressor routinely directs physical aggression at the target is still dominance aggression. An insult made in an online post visible to other members of the class is still rejective aggression. A photo showing an aggressor and her friends having fun without the target shared via a social media app to a group that includes the target is still relational aggression. In other words, social media is a virtual expressive means of communicating aggression. Other means include direct communication (face-to-face), indirect communication (rumors, talking behind someone's back), and physical expressive communication (writing, pictures on physical objects). Directing aggression at a target using technology does not make it a different type of aggression.

A more accurate way to describe an instance of cyberbullying would be to say, for example, "dominance aggression using intimidating texts" or "a relational aggression campaign conducted using Snapchat and Instagram." The application or social media channel used is incidental to the aggression itself. Classifying cyberbullying not as a type of bullying but rather as a means of delivering aggression is not meant to diminish its significance in bullying. It is meant to avoid a common pitfall of focusing on the technology and not the type of aggression delivered using the technology.

While cyberbullying is not a different type of aggression, social media is exceptionally effective as a delivery method for aggression and is problematic for the following reasons:

- **constant contact:** social media allows students to interact constantly, even at times when direct communication is not permitted or possible. Social media essentially creates unrestricted social time, which is when most bullying tends to occur.
- **broad audience:** social media provides a constant peer audience, which is both a benefit and a convenience since aggression to positively affect social status requires such an audience.
- **addictive:** social media is addictive. Even students who are harmed by aggression delivered via social media are unable to ignore it. Social media essentially eliminates the ability of targets to separate from their aggressors.
- **invisible to adults:** aggression delivered via social media can be invisible to adults. Unless adults are monitoring the social media of students, they may be completely unaware of harmful aggression that is occurring in their presence.
- **anonymity:** aggressors and supporters are able to use social media to direct aggression at others while remaining anonymous, which can make resolution efforts particularly challenging.

Who Can Determine When Bullying Occurs

Because aggression that causes harm can be indistinguishable from aggression that doesn't cause harm, only the target can determine when bullying occurs. Bullying is determined based on how the target *feels*, not how the aggressor acts or how the target reacts.

Adults cannot determine when bullying occurs from either the behavior of the aggressor or the visible reaction of the target. An aggressor may direct identical behaviors at multiple targets, but not every target will be harmed. And targets may get angry or appear bothered by the aggression but are not necessarily harmed. Conversely, some targets who appear to be completely unaffected by aggression may be significantly harmed.

Adults can, however, deduce when a target is likely being harmed from observable aggression based on the target's social position in the peer group, the size of the target's social network, and whether or not a target embraces unmonitored social time or tries to avoid it. In addition, adults can suspect that harm has started to occur to a student targeted by aggression based on observed changes like a decline in grades, lack of sleep, complaints of physical ailments, a sudden desire not to be with peers (especially during unmonitored social time), and a change in demeanor. Since these changes can also indicate some other emotional event in the student's life, adults need to get confirmation from the target. However, these indicators do provide an opportunity for adults to engage in a conversation with the student to determine if bullying is occurring (or, of course, if the student has some other issue for which adults can provide help and support).

That targets are the only ones who can determine if bullying is occurring is a concept that some adults may find challenging to accept due to the traditional way bullying problems are handled. In traditional approaches where bullying is addressed through punitive consequences, having a target determine when bullying is occurring means that the target, not an administrator, would then determine when a peer is to be punished. That is why traditional approaches require an investigation first by an administrator before a determination on bullying is made. However, since punitive consequences are ineffective and frequently counterproductive in stopping bullying and are not used in this Method, administrators should feel comfortable and confident relying on the word of the target to determine whether bullying is occurring.

That is not to say that investigations are never necessary. An issue that has been ongoing for some time and involves multiple aggressors may require an investigation to determine the full extent of aggressor and supporter involvement. And determining the roles different students are playing in the bullying (aggressor, supporter, bystander) is important for getting the aggression to stop. However, a target who admits to being harmed has confirmed that bullying is occurring and thus has rendered an investigation for the purpose of establishing that fact unnecessary.

Principles of Target Empowerment: Reacting vs. Responding

Aggression can provide a social benefit to the aggressor no matter how the target reacts. However, a target's reaction to aggression can make the aggression even more successful at providing a benefit. For example, a target who gets visibly upset at an insult can make the aggression more entertaining for observing peers, earning increased admiration for the aggressor. And a reaction that increases the social benefit increases the likelihood that the aggression will be repeated. Dominance aggression actually requires the target to react in a certain way (showing fear or explicit deference) in order to be successful.

However, students can learn ways to thoughtfully *respond* to aggression to reduce or eliminate the benefits, improving the chances that it won't be repeated. Some responses can even cause the aggression to result in a social status cost to the aggressor, which generally guarantees that it won't be repeated.

The following empowerment principles, which are described in detail in chapter 10 and illustrated in the student guide, should be discussed with targets who seek adult help and support:

- In **dominance aggression**, aggressors use threats and intimidation to instill fear in a target. The normal and natural *reaction* of a target when faced with a threat of harm is to exhibit fear and/or show deference, which allows the aggressor to gain the respect of those watching. If the target *responds* to dominance aggression by not showing fear, even if the target is afraid, the aggressor does not earn respect from the peer audience. An aggressor using dominance aggression against a target who appears unaffected can actually lose social status because the target is showing peers that the aggressor is not someone to fear and whose intimidation can be ignored.

- In **rejective aggression**, aggressors use insults, mocking, or antagonism to indicate a difference between the aggressor and target by diminishing or demeaning a particular characteristic. In this type of aggression, the aggressor may be trying to appear clever and entertaining to peers. When an insult, for example, makes peers laugh, the aggressor may gain social status no matter how the target reacts. If the target *reacts* by getting visibly upset, the aggression may be even more entertaining to peers and increase the social benefit. However, if the target *responds* by joining in and laughing or explicitly showing that the aggression is not hurtful, the aggressor may not gain status and can even lose status.

- In **relational aggression**, the aggressor starts a campaign to get members of the target's peer group to stop being friends with the target. When a target becomes aware of such a campaign, her natural *reaction* is to hope or pretend that it isn't happening. This inaction allows the aggressor to conduct the bullying campaign without interference until the target is left socially isolated. A target must *respond* by taking immediate action to find out who is behind the campaign and why. The target can then try to address any conflict that may have caused the campaign or try to understand the reason for the aggression and diffuse it. The target can also ask participants to help by not joining the side of the aggressor.

Although thoughtful responses to aggression can reduce or eliminate the social benefits and the likelihood the aggression will be repeated, not every target will be able to respond in these ways. The nature and composition of the peer group can also make these responses ineffective. Some students may need to practice the responses a few times before they see results.

Please note that ignoring aggression is not considered a thoughtful response. A thoughtful response requires an acknowledgment of the aggression and a follow-up action by the target, one that deprives the aggressor of a social benefit. Target empowerment is described in detail in chapter 10.

Principles of Bystander Empowerment

Like targets, bystanders can also take action to prevent and stop bullying. Not only can they change the outcome of a bullying incident, but they also can make aggression less accepted within the group itself. A bystander who intervenes on behalf of a target sends a message to others that the target is someone who is valued and that the aggression is unacceptable. Intervention can also increase the social status of the target, particularly if the peer who intervened is very popular. The target may be seen as a friend of the peer who intervened, and any further aggression against the target would carry greater social risk.

Bystander intervention, however, is risky for the student taking action. Students who intervene may lose status or may become a target themselves. Even though bystanders may not like what they see, these risks make them reluctant to act. They don't want to be seen by peer group members as taking the side of a lower-status target against a higher-status aggressor or taking action that is contrary to what is acceptable to the group.

Bystanders can intervene in two general ways: directly and indirectly. Direct intervention is when a bystander interrupts an instance of aggression in progress and asks the aggressor to stop. The bystander acts as a defender, visible to the target, aggressor, and those watching or participating. Direct intervention is confrontational and carries significant social risk and risk of becoming a target because the bystander is generally siding with a less popular student against a more popular student. Because of this risk, adults should never ask a student to directly intervene in a bullying problem. Direct intervention is a personal choice that only a student can make.

Indirect intervention is far less risky than direct intervention. In indirect intervention, bystanders do not publicly confront the aggressor with peers watching. Instead, the bystander takes action in private or quietly works to increase the social status of the target. Examples of indirect intervention include interrupting and stopping bullying in progress but pretending to be unaware it is happening, talking to the aggressor in private to let him know the bullying is unacceptable, and befriending the target and including the target in social activities.

Bystander empowerment is described in detail in chapter 10.

Stopping Harmful Aggression

Given that aggression provides a social benefit and that aggressors may continue the aggression even when they are aware of the harm due to that social benefit, the solution to stopping harmful aggression is to ensure that the outcome of the aggression is a negation of the benefit or even a social status cost to the aggressor. Educators, parents, and students can take actions that negate the benefit or impose a social cost:

- **educators:** the Constructive Consequences, Chain of Custody Awareness, and Classroom Strategies mechanisms are all designed to either impose a social cost or negate the benefit of aggression. Partnership with parents also plays a role in ensuring a negative social impact. Subsequent chapters in this guide will describe these mechanisms in detail.

- **students:** learning ways to thoughtfully respond to aggression can reduce or eliminate the benefits that it provides, ensuring it will cease. However, the effectiveness of responses depends on a number of variables. Chapter 10 describes how students can effectively respond to bullying in more detail.

- **parents:** all parents should learn about the drivers and mechanics of bullying so they will understand that the acknowledgment of aggression by their own child is not an indictment of their child's character, that their child may not be intending to harm a peer, and that the behavior needs to stop. Constructive parent involvement is critical to ensure aggression does not continue outside of school, whether physically or virtually. Parents can take actions that impose a social cost for continued aggression. Chapter 11 describes in more detail the roles of parents in working in partnership with educators to get bullying to stop.

Staff Education
Additional Considerations

3

> **Overview:** While chapter 2 describes the fundamentals of bullying, this chapter provides information on additional concepts related to bullying that staff can use to deepen their understanding of the topic and to make their actions to prevent and resolve issues more effective.

Students Are Both Aggressors and Targets

All students use aggression, including those with the lowest status, and all students are targets of aggression, including the most popular students. Not all targets, however, are harmed by aggression. No student is only an aggressor or only a target.

Bullying Is Not "Being Mean"

To an observer, the aggressions that students use to positively affect social status can appear to be mean and cruel. However, it is critical to remember that cruelty is generally not the intent. The aggressor is not thinking about the effect the behavior has on the target; the aggressor is focused on how the peer audience perceives the behavior and if the aggression provides a status benefit.

Targets Simply Want the Behavior to Stop

In most cases, targets of aggression do not want aggressors to receive punitive consequences. Targets simply want the aggression to stop. Stopping the aggression provides a measure of relief in that the target is not subjected to overt indications of peer rejection. In addition, targets do not want others to be aware that the aggression is causing harm, which is what punishing the aggressor implies.

Targets Become Preoccupied with Harmful Aggression

A bullied student will be preoccupied with the aggression and the feeling of diminished social status and will be unable to focus on schoolwork and other activities. All students are concerned with their social status, and those who are not feeling secure in their status due to aggression will focus on trying to counter it in some way at the expense of other priorities. This makes the rapid surfacing and resolution of bullying issues critical to the health and education of targets.

"Antisocial" Students May Simply Be Seeking Acceptance

A student who has a strong need for peer approval may engage in a steady stream of aggressive behaviors in an attempt to positively affect social status and self-esteem. A student who may be the target of aggression in one social group, including family members at home, may try to compensate for decreased self-esteem and a low social status by targeting everyone in a different social or peer group. Those perceived as antisocial in school may be trying to compensate for rejection experienced outside of school. This concept is important in that resolving a behavioral or bullying issue in school may require action to get the aggression directed at the student outside of school to stop. If the aggression in school provides a social benefit to the student that is compensating for harm caused by the aggression of others outside of school, partnership with parents will be critical to effecting a behavioral change.

Bystander Participation Is Often Self-Interest

Bystanders who participate in the aggression directed by one student against another or who passively observe but don't intervene, even when the target is visibly upset, are acting in their own self-interest. Bystanders who participate are using the opportunity to gain the approval of the aggressor or to ensure that the aggressor does not make them a target. Bystanders are indicating to the peer audience that they associate themselves with and support the higher-status aggressor and not the lower-status target. The students who don't intervene are doing so for the same reason, just implicitly. While some students who witness bullying may not like what they are seeing and may feel empathy for the target, they may not act due to the social cost that standing up to the more popular aggressor would incur.

Students May Side with Popular Aggressors Over Friends

Peer approval is so important to some students that about 33% will put their personal social status as a priority over friendships. This means that about one-third of students will stand by and watch their friends be teased or mocked without intervening and will sometimes join in even when their friends are visibly upset.

Sustained Aggression Normalizes the Treatment of a Target

A target who is repeatedly subjected to aggression by a peer group will become more rejected by that group over time. Eventually, peers will view the target as deserving of the treatment. They will view the aggression directed at the target simply as the normal way the group interacts with this person. Large peer groups such as a class will commonly have one or two such chronically targeted students.

Characteristics of Chronically Targeted Students Influence Peer Group Preferences

The personal characteristics of chronically targeted students will influence peer group preferences in that peer group members will not want to be associated with individuals who have the same characteristics as the targets. Members of the peer group will direct aggression at anyone with a similar characteristic. For example, a new student who joins the class and shares a characteristic with a chronically targeted student will likely be automatically rejected by the peer group or may have a harder time being accepted and making friends. A new student may feel compelled to direct aggression at the chronically targeted student simply to demonstrate agreement with peers in rejecting that characteristic in order to gain peer acceptance.

Students Do Not Consider Their Own Behavior to Be Bullying

Students do not always make a connection between bullying discussed as a concept and the aggression that occurs within their peer groups. This occurs for a variety of reasons:

* Students direct aggression at many individuals in order to gain social status; their focus is not on how the individuals are feeling but on whether they themselves are benefitting socially.
* Targets often pretend to be unaffected by the aggression, so aggressors don't always have a clear, visible indicator that their behavior is causing harm.
* The concept that identical behavior can result in harm in some cases but not others can be difficult for some students to grasp. From the perspective of the aggressor, the aggression directed at an unharmed student is no different in action and intent from the same behavior directed at a student who suffers harm.
* When aggression is directed by members of a peer group at individuals outside the group, the aggression is viewed as assertion of the group identity (again, the effect on the target is not considered).
* When students direct aggression at a target over a long period of time, students may view the aggression simply as the normal way to treat the target. Sustained bullying desensitizes

students to their own behavior. Students who vocally profess to being strongly against bullying will not recognize that their own aggression toward a long-time target is bullying.

- The term "bullying" is frequently misused to describe aggression that results in "bothering" (annoyance, aggravation, frustration, etc.) and not harm. Students need to be taught the difference between the two, specifically that being bothered by aggression is not the same as being harmed by it. Students who proclaim to be "bullied" by another in the presence of peers or directly accuse a peer of bullying them are more likely to mean that they are "bothered" and not emotionally harmed. Those who truly feel rejected by peers tend not to acknowledge that rejection in front of peers.

Aggression Initiated Due to a Positive Characteristic

A positive characteristic of a student, such as a talent, an achievement, a desirable material possession, or an attractive attribute can cause that student to be targeted by aggression. A positive characteristic can boost the status of the student or can disrupt the established social order and may make other students feel that their own status is threatened.

Positive characteristics often drive relational aggression campaigns. The positive characteristic of the target makes the aggressor fearful that her own popularity and friendships are at risk due to the increased social status that this characteristic provides the target. In response to these fears, an aggressor may launch a campaign to get others to abandon their friendships with the target, leaving the target socially isolated and with a diminished social status. This decrease in the social status of the target reassures the aggressor that her social position is secure. A relational aggression campaign that is initiated due to a sudden positive change—such as the target winning a contest, getting a fancy new car, or being named as the captain of a sports team—can be extremely disorienting to the target in terms of the sudden loss of friendships and isolation.

Relational Aggression Initiated Due to a Personal Offense

One driver of relational aggression campaigns is when the aggressor feels offended by the target but does not want to address the offense directly. Instead, the aggressor uses relational aggression to get back at or punish the target. One reason the aggressor avoids direct confrontation is fear that doing so may result in a loss of the friendship. The aggressor views the use of relational aggression as safer since it provides a feeling of justice while minimizing the risk of friendship loss. While the aggressor in these cases may only intend to temporarily affect the friendships of the target, it can result in permanent social damage.

Lack of Adult Intervention Is Viewed as Tacit Approval

Students will assume that adults who do not stop aggression that they witness condone the behavior. The failure of adults to intervene in cases of harmful aggression will, over time, contribute to normalizing the bullying. Adults need to identify cases of harmful aggression, particularly chronically targeted students, so they can intervene to demonstrate that they don't condone the behavior, help the aggressors realize that their behavior is harmful, and help reverse the harm caused to the target.

Educators Can Set a Negative Tone

Educators' own reactions to students, specifically expressions of annoyance or negative feelings, can result in a student becoming a target of aggression. When students see an educator acting negatively toward a student, they may perceive that as permission to do the same. Students who seek that educator's approval may also target the student because they think that doing so will earn that approval. Educators need to take great care to avoid making any personal negative expressions about a student.

Constructive Consequences

4

> **Overview:** The Constructive Consequences mechanism is a way of resolving a bullying problem by leveraging the same drivers of aggression to get it to stop. Aggressors are often unaware that they are causing harm. Even when told that their behavior is causing harm, the desire for the social benefit may override any concern about the harm being caused or the knowledge of the effect of the behavior. The solution is to impose a consequence that not just eliminates the social benefit but results in a social cost. The consequence doesn't actually have to be imposed to get the aggression to stop; the aggressor's fear of losing social status will often be enough to stop the behavior.

Background

The challenges with traditional bullying prevention approaches are numerous and described in appendix B; however, they are worth briefly mentioning here since they help to frame why the Constructive Consequences mechanism is so effective.

In a traditional approach, a student is accused of bullying another. The word "bully" immediately puts the aggressor and his parents on the defensive since the word carries negative connotations about character. In addition, from the perspective of the aggressor, the accusation is false because he is not bullying; he is just treating the other student the way peers treat the student and no differently than he treats other students, including friends. Worried about being punished, the aggressor tries to justify his behavior by blaming the target for instigating it or for also using aggression. If the school has a traditional bullying reporting mechanism such as an online form, the aggressor (and sometimes his parents) blames the target for "tattling" or being the instigator.

The principal investigates and reaches a judgment that inevitably results in the dissatisfaction of all involved and likely makes the problem worse. If the principal finds for the target, that bullying is occurring, she then punishes the aggressor. The aggressor perceives the punishment as an injustice and retaliates against the target, and the aggressor's parents are furious with the school.

In addition, the punishment itself can serve to boost the status of the aggressor among peers, which then reinforces the bullying. The problem is now worse for the target.

If the principal judges that the target, who is suffering harm, is not really being bullied, or for whatever reason doesn't want to impose the punitive consequence on the aggressor, the target suffers further injury in not being believed, and the principal has implicitly given the aggressor permission to continue the bullying, which infuriates the target's parents. Not only will the bullying continue for the target, but he will feel trapped in an abusive relationship with no constructive way out. And the principal has just increased the school's liability risk for any negative or tragic outcome of the bullying.

In short, the traditional approach makes the problem worse for the target, results in an antagonistic relationship with one or both sets of parents, is a wasted teaching opportunity not only to help the aggressor understand the harm of his behavior but also to empower the target, and sets the school up for liability if there is a bad outcome. After all the time and effort, the problem is generally either not solved or made worse. The target's suffering continues but now carries an added risk that the target may feel desperation, and the aggressor is none the wiser about the harmful effects of his behavior.

How Constructive Consequences Works

Constructive Consequences solves the problems inherent in the traditional bullying prevention approach. When a bullying problem is identified, the principal learns from the target what the aggressor and any supporters are doing and where it is occurring. Because the principal will not be punishing the aggressor, she is able to take the target at his word about the aggressor and any supporters' behaviors. For the purpose of the conversation with the aggressor, however, she gets confirmation from the educators who are with the aggressor and target during the day that these behaviors are occurring.

The principal then initiates a conversation with the aggressor where she emphasizes that he is a good person but his behavior is causing harm (focus is on behavior, not character). She notes that the behavior has been observed by adults in order to prevent the aggressor from blaming the target. She further explains how aggression can harm some people but not others, and in this case it is causing harm. She emphasizes that it is okay if the aggressor did not realize that he was causing harm; his goal was to entertain friends or to look good in front of peers, to gain peer approval, etc., and he wasn't thinking about the effect of his behavior on the target. So he wasn't doing anything wrong. Now, however, he has been informed that his behavior is causing harm and the behavior must stop. If the behavior continues, then he will be doing something wrong, namely, intentionally causing harm, for which there will be a consequence.

If the school has implemented the Student Education and Empowerment mechanism (described in chapter 10), then the conversation at this point serves as a refresher to the student. Otherwise, the student has just received an education on bullying. The student now understands that the conversation is about his behavior and not his character. He is relieved to know that he will not be punished for the behavior since the principal accepts that he may not have realized that his behavior is causing harm. And he does not feel antagonistic toward the target since he understands that adults observed the behavior and are calling him out for it.

The principal now presents the aggressor with an opportunity to stop his behavior in order to avoid a consequence. The consequence is determined by where the aggression occurs. If the aggression has been occurring in person, then a continuation of the aggression will result in the aggressor being removed from the specific environment in which the behavior occurred. For example, if the aggression occurs at lunch, the aggressor will not be permitted to eat with his peer group. The student does not lose the activity (such as lunch or recess) but rather loses the coveted peer engagement that occurs with the activity. If the aggression has been occurring virtually, the aggressor will not be allowed to use social media during the school day. Further, his parents will be informed of the problem and will be asked to support the social media restriction.

The principal can also tell the aggressor that any continued aggression means that bullying is occurring, which may trigger actions mandated by the school or district and that are beyond the principal's control. She will be required to report on the incident and may be required to impose a punishment, both of which she would prefer to avoid. She can ask the aggressor to help her avoid having to carry out these steps, a use of the classic "good cop/bad cop" routine to help influence the behavioral change.

The aggressor is then informed that all adults in the school who are with the aggressor during the day will be notified about the problem and will be watching to ensure the behavior toward the target does not continue (the Chain of Custody Awareness mechanism, described in chapter 5). This is a gentle warning that the adults will be watching and will report the behavior, and the consequence will be applied. The principal also says that she will be checking in with the target to see if the aggression has continued or shifted to social media. If the behavior has stopped, then no further action will be taken.

At the conclusion of the conversation, the principal reiterates that the student is a good person and that she believes he will do the right thing and stop the behavior toward the target. As soon as possible after the conversation ends, the principal initiates Chain of Custody Awareness and, after a day or so, checks in with the target to see if the aggression has stopped. If no further aggression toward the target is reported by an adult in the chain of custody or by the target after a few days, then the matter is essentially closed. If the aggression is reported, then the principal needs to apply the consequence.

Why Constructive Consequences Works

What makes this mechanism effective is that students perceive a separation or disconnection from peers during unrestricted social time as carrying a social cost. A student who is the leader of a peer group will have anxiety that his separation from the group could result in someone else taking his place. His separation from his peers won't allow him to maintain or defend his status. Students separated from peers will feel like they are missing out and will fear that peer group changes during their absence will harm their own social standing. Those students who need constant peer approval and validation of status are often desperate to be with their peers and will do whatever they can to preserve that time with them. The strong desire of students to be with their peers will often provide the incentive to stop the behavior directed at one student in order to avoid separation. And if the aggressor's peers are his supporters, he will show disapproval if they continue to direct aggression at the target, which should get the supporters' behavior to change and avoid the need for engagement with the principal.

Other aspects of the mechanism help to drive effectiveness. The principal's emphasis that the student is good but the behavior is the problem helps the student feel that the principal believes in him and cares, which may make the principal's approval important to the student. Since aggressors are generally unaware that harm is occurring, the mechanism serves to educate the aggressor on how his behavior is affecting that one individual. The student is relieved at not being punished, and the lack of an immediate consequence means that the aggressor has no reason to blame the target, deny the behavior, try to justify the behavior, or retaliate against the target. The student may also feel a sense of heightened maturity in that he has not been given a punishment or an ultimatum but rather a choice. The principal mentioning that adults observed the behavior has made the student realize that his behavior was not going unnoticed or that the lack of intervention didn't mean that his teachers and administrators implicitly condoned it. Any student who cares about what his teachers think of him will want to stop behavior of which they disapprove. The principal asking for his help in avoiding mandated actions such as district reporting also can make the student feel good about doing the principal a "favor." And being told that all adults who are with the student and the target during the school day will be watching to ensure that the behavior has stopped provides an additional incentive for the student to comply with a pledge to change behavior and avoid the consequence.

Parent Engagement

Parent engagement is always at the discretion of the administration. However, one benefit of Constructive Consequences is that bullying problems can often be resolved from just the conversation with the aggressor, which means that parent engagement is often not necessary. Since the aggressor is not suffering a punitive consequence, the principal does not need to take the time to explain why the student is being punished or to address the concerns of upset parents. In addition, if the aggression had been conducted over social media but stops, then the principal does not need to enlist the help of the aggressor's parents to restrict social media access. Further, given the way targets will start reporting bullying issues when this Method is adopted—directly and informally—the principal will not need to respond to a formal bullying reporting form that has been submitted by the target's parents.

If the parents of the aggressor are engaged, such as to help enforce a social media restriction, then the principal has an opportunity to explain that the issue is about behavior and not about character, and any consequence that was applied was due solely to an intentional act by their child in continuing a behavior after being informed about the harm it was causing, not due to administrative judgment. That puts responsibility for the consequence on the child and not the school. Administrators should also strongly recommend that parents refrain from applying punitive consequences at home since this can be counterproductive.

In cases where the target has suffered significant harm, the target's parents can be made aware of the situation. Further, awareness may help the target's parents to understand any recent behavioral changes or decline in academic performance. Notification of the target's parents also allows them to provide additional support to the target to recover from the harm. If the target's parents demand some form of justice, the principal can explain that targets generally do not want punitive consequences applied since it can make the problem worse through retaliation and it can increase peer awareness of the problem.

Please note that targets often prefer that parents not know about a bullying problem, particularly if the target's parents are from a culture in which being a target is considered a weakness and would be met with disapproval. Administrators should ask the target if he wants his parents to know. If, in the judgment of administration, notification is necessary due to the harm caused, the administration should let the target know that his parents will be notified in advance of that notification.

Stakeholder Benefits

Constructive Consequences tends to leave everyone involved satisfied:

* **Targets** benefit because the process usually stops the aggression immediately, eliminates the risk of retaliation from the aggressor for being punished, and prevents the target from being blamed for reporting the problem. Targets also feel safe knowing that adults are aware and watching, and they can take comfort that the aggressor will be removed from the environment

if the aggression continues. Further, they take additional comfort when the principal checks in to see if the aggression has stopped.

- **Targets' parents**, if they are engaged, are satisfied because the bullying often stops immediately. The principal can also help them to understand the perspective of the aggressor, specifically that the harm to their child was not intentional. Those parents who demand some form of justice for the bullying become satisfied once they understand that their child does not want the aggressor to be punished but simply wants the bullying to stop.
- **Aggressors** are satisfied since they are able to avoid a consequence by changing their behavior toward one individual. They also learn how their aggression can harm others. Further, they become aware that adults believe in them and are observing their behavior, which can become a driver of positive change in order to secure adult approval. They also learn that adults do not condone the behavior, which, in aggregate, results in a positive change to the overall school climate.
- **Aggressors' parents**, if they are engaged, are satisfied since their child isn't being "unfairly" punished and are satisfied that the process is simply a behavioral change exercise. Further, they understand that whether their child suffers a consequence is not due to adult judgment or the target's word but depends entirely upon their child's actions.
- **Educators** often see immediate and complete resolution of bullying problems without the need for a consequence and realize significant time savings in not having to conduct lengthy investigations, meet with parents in every case, or manage persisting bullying problems.

A final but quite significant benefit of a nonpunitive consequence to stop bullying is that it removes the barrier to student reporting of bullying problems. Constructive Consequences eliminates the social cost of reporting since telling adults about problems will not get peers in trouble. This concept is described in chapter 7.

Preparing for the Conversation with the Aggressor

When the principal becomes aware of a bullying problem by a target who requests help, she can either immediately engage the aggressor or first have the educators who are with the aggressor and target observe them to confirm the aggression. A delay in engaging the aggressor is not necessary but it can be helpful. Confirmation of the aggression is helpful when the principal tells the aggressor that the aggression was not reported by the target but observed by adults. However, if the target is desperate for the aggression to stop, the principal should not wait. The principal should discuss this with the target to determine if a target is willing to endure additional aggression for a day or two knowing that the principal is aware of the problem and is taking action.

Target Support at the Time of Reporting

A request for help by a target and the discussion with the principal about the aggression also present an opportunity for the principal to educate and empower the target. The conversation with the target who reports the problem should follow the Five-Step Framework (described in chapter 6) with the goals of repairing the harm caused by the aggression and empowering the target to deal with future instances of aggression (described in chapter 10). However, care must be taken NOT to give the target the impression that administration won't be taking action and is simply redirecting the target to empowerment. A target who asks for help needs adult intervention.

Aggressor Discussion Outline

The following discussion outline provides the key points to cover in order to ensure success:

1. **Start on a positive note.** The principal can mention something positive the student has done or ask how he is doing in a particular class or extracurricular activity to make a personal connection and to demonstrate caring for the student. This helps reinforce that the conversation is not about the student but rather about behavior.

2. **Discuss the behavior.** State that adults have observed the student using aggression toward one particular student and that the aggression is causing harm. Mention the times and places the aggression has been observed.

3. **Make the aggressor aware that the target is being harmed.** Let the aggressor know that the behavior directed at the target is causing emotional harm. Explain that while some peers who face that type of aggression are not harmed, this particular peer is being harmed.

4. **Let the aggressor explain.** Let the aggressor tell his side of the story, i.e., provide any rationale for his actions. Letting the aggressor explain not only makes him feel valued but also may uncover an underlying conflict or other issue that is driving the aggression. The aggressor may reveal that he is being bullied by another student or adult for which the aggression being discussed is a symptom. Letting the aggressor explain allows the conversation to move past any attempts at denial or justifications. The aggressor may also surface instances where the aggression is a response to behaviors by the target, which can allow administrators to address both problems.

5. **Review the facts about aggression.** Talk about how students use aggressive behavior without the intent to harm and how that may in fact be happening in this case. Talk about how targets try to hide how they feel about aggression, which further prevents aggressors from knowing they are causing harm. Let the aggressor know that he is not being judged for using the aggression or being accused of intentionally harming the target. It is simply the case that harm is occurring.

6. **If possible, humanize the target.** During the conversation, talk about the target to help the aggressor see the target as a person, especially in cases where the aggressor is using a general characteristic of the target in the bullying, such as ethnicity, skin color, or gender identity.

7. **State that the behavior toward the target must stop.** Let the aggressor know that there will be no consequence if the aggression directed at the target stops. The request to stop aggression is limited to that one target. If the aggression toward that individual stops, there is no further conversation on the topic and the matter is considered resolved. However, if the aggressive behavior directed at that individual continues, there will be a consequence.

8. **Explain the consequence.** Let the aggressor know that if the behavior continues, he will be removed from the same environment as the target during the times that the aggression has been observed. If the aggression happens in the cafeteria, the aggressor will eat lunch apart from his peers. If it happens on the playground, the aggressor will be separated from his peers or may need to have recess in a different location if separation on the playground is not possible. If the aggression was delivered via social media, then access to social media will be restricted during school time and, further, his parents will be notified in order to help enforce the restriction outside of school. Give the aggressor a moment to think about what it would mean to be separated from his peers. Ensure the aggressor understands that whether the consequence is applied is entirely up to him based on his own behavior. He can avoid the consequence and potential parental notification simply by stopping the behavior. It's that easy.

9. **Explain any mandatory actions triggered by bullying.** Explain how aggression that causes harm is classified as bullying and that now that the aggressor is aware that his behavior is causing harm, any further instances of the aggression would be considered intentional bullying. Explain any actions mandated by the district in response to bullying, such as district notification or reporting, punishment, contacting parents, etc. Emphasize that if the behavior stops, no action will be taken because the aggressor was simply unaware of the harm he was causing, but if the behavior continues, the aggressor will be intentionally bullying and the school will have no choice but to take these mandated steps. The principal can position this explanation as asking for the aggressor's help in avoiding all the mandatory actions; it allows the aggressor to feel as though he is doing the principal a favor by changing his behavior.

10. **Emphasize the choice.** On the one hand, the aggressor can simply stop the aggression directed at a single individual and the matter is settled. Or the aggressor can continue and: 1. he will face the consequence; 2. his parents will be notified; 3. district requirements will apply; and 4. if policy requires, a punitive consequence may also be applied.

11. **Empathize about how hard the choice might seem.** Relay an understanding that it can be difficult for a student who uses such behaviors to stop those behaviors, but express confidence that the aggressor can do it.

12. **Get commitment from the aggressor to stop.** Have the aggressor explicitly state that he will stop the aggressive behavior toward that one target. Emphasize the fact that there will be no consequence if the behavior stops.

13. **Thank the aggressor for his commitment to change.** Let the aggressor know that he is helping to solve the problem.

14. **Explain Chain of Custody Awareness.** Let the aggressor know that to ensure the behavior stops, all the adults the aggressor is with during the day will be made aware of the problem and will be observing interactions with the target to ensure the behavior does not continue. Let the aggressor know that this is standard procedure. Emphasize that if one of these adults reports an instance of aggression, then the consequence will be applied. Have the aggressor acknowledge again his understanding that continued use of aggression toward the target will trigger the consequence.

15. **End on a positive note.** Express trust and faith in the aggressor to make this positive change in behavior toward this one individual.

Chain of Custody Awareness Initiation and Target Notification

After the conversation with the aggressor, the principal should do two things. First, initiate Chain of Custody Awareness, which is described in detail in chapter 5. This mechanism involves notifying all the educators who are with both the aggressor and target during the school day to immediately start monitoring the aggressor and his friends and supporters for any aggression directed at the target. If educators observe any aggression, they should stop it, document it, and report it immediately.

The second action the principal should take is to inform the target that the conversation with the aggressor has taken place; that the aggressor has pledged to stop; that the educators who are with the aggressor and target during the day have been informed of the problem and will be keeping watch; and that the target should report any further instances of aggression to the principal, including preserving evidence of the use of social media (e.g., screenshots).

If there are no reports of further aggression after a reasonable period (a few days should be sufficient) and the target confirms that the aggression has stopped, the matter will be considered resolved. The administrator will update the Chain of Custody Awareness notification mechanism to indicate that monitoring of the aggressor and target can stop. The principal can also thank the aggressor for making a positive change. However, if the aggression continues, the consequence should be applied.

Applying the Consequence

If the aggression has continued, the principal should have a frank discussion with the aggressor about the reports of continued aggression and the previously discussed consequence that would occur in such circumstances, including any additional required actions (e.g., district bullying report). The principal can proceed in a measured fashion. She can apply the constructive consequence and see if that addresses the problem. If the aggression does not resume when the aggressor rejoins his peer group, the matter is considered closed. If the aggression continues, the consequence is reapplied and the principal notifies the aggressor's parents. The principal can again express faith that the behavior can change and ask the aggressor for a commitment to do so, and also warn that further aggression will trigger required district reporting and punitive consequences.

Constructive Consequences for Relational Aggression

Constructive Consequences may not be as effective in stopping relational aggression because a target may not even become aware of the aggression until after the damage to friendships is complete and the campaign has essentially finished. In other words, by the time a target comes forward to seek help, the aggression may have already stopped. In addition, relational aggression does not always involve behaviors in front of a peer audience that can be observed like dominance and rejective aggression. The behaviors involved in relational aggression are often peer-to-peer or are witnessed only by members of the peer group.

While stopping the behavior in cases of dominance and rejective aggression provides immediate relief to targets, reversing the harm caused by relational aggression requires a sincere effort by the aggressor. How sincere this effort would be if mandated as a consequence is questionable given that reversing the damage might result in a reduction of the aggressor's own social status. However, the aggressor should be asked to make a best effort to undo the harm she caused.

Given the lack of a direct connection between removal from the environment and relational aggression, administration should make a decision about each case based on the circumstances. One option is to examine whether social media was used in the aggression. If so, a loss of social media access for a time should be considered as a consequence. Due to the covert nature of this type of aggression, parent notification may be required to enlist help in getting the aggression to stop.

In all cases of relational aggression, where the result is social isolation of the target (a complete severing of the target's friendships), target support is critical. The target will need empathy and emotional support from all adults in her life, including parents, while she reestablishes her place in the larger peer group by forming or joining a new circle of friends.

Consequences for Cyberbullying

In all cases, administrators should determine if any aggression occurred via social media. If so, a consequence of further aggression via social media should be a restriction on using social media. Since using social media is covert and won't be visible to adults in the chain of custody, administration should ask targets to report any instances of cyberbullying and, if possible, provide evidence (e.g., screenshots or emails). A constructive consequence that involves removal from the physical environment becomes ineffective if the aggressor is able to maintain virtual contact with peers via social media.

If an aggressor continues to use social media as a means of delivering aggression, the aggressor's access to social media must be restricted. This can include a prohibition on bringing electronic devices to school, surrendering them if brought to school, and loss of online access. If aggression via social media continues after the initial aggressor engagement such that a consequence must be applied, administration should contact the aggressor's parents to enlist their help in enforcing a restriction on social media outside of school.

Reasons for the Aggression

How easily the aggressor is able to change his behavior may depend upon why the aggressor is using the behavior. The conversation with the aggressor should try to identify the reason for the aggression since additional steps may be necessary to get the behavior to stop. Reasons can include the following:

- **opportunity for status improvement:** in these cases, typical of dominance and rejective aggression, the aggressor is simply trying to achieve a social status improvement by using behaviors in front of a peer audience. These cases should be the most common and generally should resolve without any additional steps.
- **retaliation:** aggressors may be using aggression to get back at a target for an actual or perceived offense. Administrators may need to help the aggressor and target resolve the underlying conflict.
- **bullying driven by bullying:** an aggressor may be targeting a student in response to or in compensation for being bullied. Administrators must address the bullying of the aggressor in parallel with the request to the aggressor to change behavior. Stopping the bullying of the aggressor may resolve both problems.
- **bullying driven by contempt:** these cases are challenging since the aggressor may feel justified in using the bullying behavior. The aggressor may not see the target as a person but rather only see the characteristic for which the aggressor feels contempt, a feeling that may even be reinforced by peer group norms. Aggressors need to be taught to respect the target's

characteristic that the aggressor uses to justify aggressive behavior, no matter what peers think. Administrators may also need to take steps to humanize the target in the eyes of the aggressor and peer group.

- **bullying to eliminate a perceived social threat:** as mentioned above, relational aggression cases are challenging to resolve since the aggressor considers her own social status to be threatened by the target. The aggressor feels justified in using relational aggression because she is simply responding to the threat posed by the target. The aggressor may not feel secure until the status of the target has been diminished. An aggressor may have a hard time accepting a positive characteristic of a target where that characteristic boosts the social status of the target. Additional support (e.g., psychologist or counselor) may also be helpful in cases where the aggressor's need for status makes her unable to stop the behavior.

Additional Considerations

Administrators Must Approach Bullying Issues Objectively

One aspect of bullying that makes resolution challenging is that the aggressors are often students who are not just popular with peers but are also popular with educators. The support and, at times, special or favored treatment that these popular students receive can actually make them more effective at using aggression among peers to boost their own social status.

It is perfectly normal for an administrator to give a "good kid" a pass when any other student might face a consequence. It is also normal for an administrator to give more weight to the justifications of a behavior provided by that good student than by any other student. However, what is critical to remember in bullying cases, even those involving a popular student, is that another student is suffering emotional harm. In other words, the popular student is perpetrating "invisible violence" against the target. No matter how "good" or "admirable" the student is, how easy the student makes things for administrators, or how much the student's achievements in athletics, academics, music, or other activity reflect positively on the school, administrators must put these feelings aside and address the bullying problem objectively. Good students should not get a free pass for causing harm. Any subjectivity of this type that enters into the bullying resolution process will undermine the entire approach and credibility of administrators. If students become aware that some students, particularly the popular ones who set the tone for aggression and perpetrate it, are being treated differently and are actually receiving support from educators, the students will lose trust in the administration to effectively and fairly deal with bullying issues. Further, favoritism or unequal application of bullying prevention measures could increase a school's liability risk.

Ensure No Punishment for the Target

The consequence for continued aggression should apply to the aggressor and not the target, even if seemingly well-intentioned. Specifically, the target should not be the one to be removed from the environment unless at the explicit request of the target. For example, a target bullied in the cafeteria should not be asked to eat in a classroom because it is "better" or "safer" for the target. Instead, the aggressor should eat elsewhere. If bullying occurs online, the target should not lose online access to "protect" the target from the aggression. It is the aggressor who should have access restricted. If bullying occurs in the classroom, it is not the target who should be made to change seats. Instead, the aggressor should be moved. A target should not have to make changes to accommodate the actions of an aggressor.

Discipline Code Violations by Targets in Response to Bullying

Just like some instances of bullying can be a reaction to being bullied (see Reasons for the Aggression, above), some violations of the discipline code by students may also be a response to bullying. A student who feels trapped in a bullying situation with no solution may lash out at the aggressor, supporters, or others by making threats, destroying property, or taking other actions that violate the discipline code. In these cases, schools should take the bullying into account when determining a consequence. More importantly, any consequences for the student who acted in response to bullying should come with a commitment from administration to deal immediately and decisively with the aggressor and any supporters to get the bullying of the target to stop. Punishing the target without also acknowledging the role that the bullying played in the target's action and putting a stop to the bullying is an injustice to the target and creates conditions for further and potentially escalating violations of the discipline code by the target.

Creative Expression Related to Bullying

Some targets use writing and art as an outlet to express their pain. Sometimes these creative expressions indicate a desire to harm peers. While schools must treat such creative expression as a warning, they should also understand that the student may have no intention of causing harm. The school should carefully and thoroughly investigate what drove the student to such expression. If, for example, a student creates a list of peers whom he wishes to harm, the school should investigate to find out what each student may have done to warrant inclusion on that list. Creative expression should always be treated as a cry for help. Schools should provide support to the target not only to heal but also to address the reason for the creative expression.

Address Group Bullying

All bullying investigations should try to determine if others are <u>directly</u> involved, i.e., active supporters, in the aggression. If stopping the behavior of the lead aggressor does not stop the aggression by supporters, they should also be held accountable. And in cases where bullying of a target in a class has persisted for some time, multiple students could be playing the role of the aggressor at different times. Students need to learn that multiple people bullying an individual does not minimize responsibility for individual action.

In addition to addressing individual bullying issues that involve multiple aggressors, administrators may want to consider breaking up peer groups that consistently engage in aggression that causes harm. For example, a peer group member can be moved to a different class. An aggressor who suddenly loses his dependable supporters and usual audience of peers loses the incentive for using the aggression. Administration may want to consider bullying problems that are proving challenging to resolve when determining class compositions at the start of each school year.

Mentor Engagement

Mentors can be engaged to talk about behavior with an aggressor if the aggressor has failed to change his behavior. Mentors can include a favorite teacher, coach, or extracurricular activity organizer. A mentor may be able to influence the aggressor to change.

However, mentors, especially those from outside the school, must have an understanding of bullying that is aligned with this Method. The mentor cannot have the attitude that bullying is just "boys being boys" or that bullying is part of growing up. And the message should not be that the student should stop the bullying to "appease the administration" or "get this problem to disappear" but rather that the behavior is harmful and must stop.

Although mentor engagement may not be an option for most students, it should be considered for cases where an aggressor is not responding to consequences and has a mentor in the school community.

Transition to Counseling

In cases where consequences are not working or where administration senses that a student may have a particularly intense need for improving status such that aggression is the student's primary form of social engagement, the aggressor may have a deeper underlying behavioral or psychological issue. The aggressor may need support from a guidance counselor, behavioral specialist, and/or school psychologist.

District Policy on Reporting and Punishment

District policies that are based on traditional definitions of bullying and traditional approaches for resolving bullying problems can, unfortunately, be counterproductive. Each principal needs to determine how to meet district reporting and punitive discipline requirements for bullying in the context of this Method.

However, if the district uses a traditional definition as the basis for policy, specifically one that defines bullying as aggression where harm is intended, the principal may be able to use that definition as the basis for decisions related to reporting and punitive consequence. If a traditional definition is used, the argument can be made that reporting and punitive discipline requirements are not triggered unless the Constructive Consequences mechanism is not effective at resolving the bullying issue. As described in chapter 2, aggressors do not intend harm but rather use aggression to positively affect social status. Only after the aggressor is informed that harm is occurring would subsequent instances of aggression meet the traditional definition of bullying. And, as all educators know, forgetful students often need reminders. Principals should be able to make the argument that aggressors may need a few reminders that harm is occurring, reminders that involve both conversations and constructive consequences, before the district's threshold for the reporting and punitive requirement is met.

In cases where a punitive consequence must be applied, a creative administrator should be able to select a punitive consequence that mirrors or has the same effect as a constructive consequence. The idea is not to bypass or ignore district policy, but simply to help ensure that the counterproductive effects of well-intentioned policies are minimized or avoided. Administrators who have any concerns about how best to support students in resolving bullying problems while also meeting district requirements may wish to consult with legal counsel.

Chain of Custody Awareness · 5

Overview: The Chain of Custody Awareness mechanism involves notifying school staff about a bullying problem so they can monitor the aggressor and target, stop aggression if they see it, and report any aggression. The "chain of custody" refers to all the staff members in a school—administrators, educators, and nonteaching support staff such as lunch and playground monitors—who are with an aggressor and a target during the school day. The mechanism provides an incentive for the aggressor to change behavior and provides the target with reassurance that staff are watching and will intervene if necessary. The Chain of Custody Awareness mechanism is generally used in tandem with the Constructive Consequences mechanism.

How Chain of Custody Awareness Works

Chain of Custody Awareness is the notification of all school staff who are with an aggressor and target during the school day about a bullying problem so staff can ensure that the aggression does not continue and, if it does, stop it, document it, and report it. This mechanism serves as a deterrent to the aggressor because he knows that adults are watching and that any reported aggression will result in a consequence. The mechanism helps the target by providing reassurance that adults are aware and will intervene if necessary. The target is also helped by knowing he can report an instance of aggression to staff who may not have witnessed it and they will understand the context and report it to administration. The mechanism makes the jobs of staff members easier since it alerts them to specific individuals who need to be monitored.

When a bullying problem is surfaced, the principal has a discussion with the aggressor about his behavior (described in chapter 4). The principal secures a commitment from the aggressor to stop the behavior that is causing harm to the target and informs him that the adults who are with him and the target during the school day will be watching to ensure that the aggression does not continue.

Following this conversation with the aggressor, the principal notifies appropriate staff so they can monitor the students involved. The notification indicates who is involved (including any supporters of the aggressor), the aggressive behavior(s) involved, and where the aggression has been occurring. Staff are asked to observe the students, intervene and stop any further instances of aggression if they see it, and report any aggression that occurs.

The time frame for heightened monitoring can vary depending upon the circumstances or can be set to a uniform time period, such as five consecutive school days or the remainder of the school week plus two days of the following week. A time period that covers the end of one school week and the beginning of the following week ensures any aggression that resumes after the weekend due to forgetfulness on the part of the aggressor is stopped. If the staff who are monitoring the students do not observe any aggression, no action is required and the monitoring can stop.

The means of communicating bullying problems to staff and reporting instances of aggression can leverage an existing method of daily communication such as a password-protected portal for staff, a daily staff briefing, or password-protected online documents. The principal may wish to directly contact staff immediately following the conversation with the aggressor to ensure that monitoring begins immediately. Whatever method is used, the information should be secure and confidential and not accessible by students. Ideally, the communication about a problem will be limited to those staff who will do the monitoring.

Chain of Custody Awareness and Cyberbullying

The visual monitoring of physical interactions, cannot, unfortunately, extend to social media. However, aggressors are warned not to use social media as a means of continuing the aggression, and targets are instructed to retain and show evidence of aggression delivered via social media to school staff. Further, the aggressor knows that any instances of reported cyberbullying will result not only in a consequence but also in parental notification. Chain of Custody Awareness ensures that staff who are presented with evidence of aggression via social media understand the context of the communication as a continuance of the aggression.

Involvement of Monitors

Staff whose role is limited to the monitoring of students, particularly during unrestricted free time, must be part of Chain of Custody Awareness. Their roles are most critical since the times they are monitoring is when aggression typically occurs. While their job responsibilities may preclude them from receiving the same level of education on bullying as the rest of the staff, they still need to understand how the Chain of Custody Awareness mechanism works and use it.

Interschool Year Chain of Custody Awareness

The end of the school year may not mean the end of a bullying problem. An unresolved bullying problem may resume the following school year. Unresolved bullying problems should be documented at the end of a school year and the information passed on to the educators who will be teaching the students the following school year. The goal is not to prejudice the educators receiving the information about the students but rather to raise awareness of a past problem that may continue.

Target Support
The Five-Step Framework

6

Overview: The Target Support mechanism consists of five steps used to guide a support discussion with a target. The discussion is designed to help the student heal, educate the student on bullying, and empower the student to take effective action to get the bullying to stop. A discussion that covers all five steps results in an action plan for resolving the bullying problem. Students choose whether they want to try to get the bullying to stop on their own or have an adult intervene. The plan provides the student with a sense of ownership of the outcome and a measure of control over the resolution process. Since each step of the discussion can be beneficial, discussions that do not cover all five steps can still be helpful to the student.

Background

Students need more from adults than just getting bullying to stop. They need a resource they can turn to when they need help, someone they can talk to about a problem and get advice from without the adult automatically taking action. While many schools have guidance personnel, a school psychologist, or other designated administrators such as the principal for students to talk to, targets sometimes won't reach out to them for a number of reasons, including the following:

- Bullying is a very personal problem, and students want to talk to someone they know and trust.
- Students who just want someone to talk to fear that a designated administrator may be required to take action such as engaging the aggressor or calling parents.
- Most students who are bullied want to solve the problem themselves in order to regain lost social status but fear that if they tell an adult, they will lose control of the problem resolution process and incur a social cost.
- Students fear that the adult they tell won't keep the conversation confidential and that, as a result, others will become aware of the problem.
- Some students may have already tried talking to an adult but did not receive effective support.

- Some students may feel that they would be stigmatized if they engaged the school counselor or psychologist.

Students would be best supported by having all staff members in the school be able to confidentially help them understand what bullying is and how it works, provide guidance on how to get bullying to stop, and help reverse the harm caused by the bullying.

Recognizing When Target Support Is Needed

One challenge for educators in knowing when a target needs support is the inability of many students to effectively communicate the seriousness of a bullying problem. Students may have difficulty finding the right words to express how much they are being harmed by the aggression of another. They frequently try to explain the problem by describing the aggressor's behavior, which, to adults, may not sound like a big deal. Adults frequently hear complaints about aggression that is not doing any actual harm, generally when one student is annoying or bothering another.

Adults must be careful not to dismiss or minimize a problem based on how the student describes the aggression. If the problem isn't a big deal, the student wouldn't be taking the risk of engaging an adult for help. And the student needs a sympathetic ear, not a dismissive one. A time-pressed adult who is asked by a student to talk privately about an interpersonal problem but then hears the student describe common aggression should not simply dismiss the student's concerns. Instead, the adult should listen carefully and ask how the aggression makes the target feel. Redirecting the conversation from the actions of the aggressor to the feelings of the target can help differentiate between aggression that is annoying and aggression that is causing harm.

The Five-Step Framework

The Target Support mechanism involves the creation of a support network for students by having all staff members learn the Five-Step Framework. The Five-Step Framework is simply an outline for a discussion with a target that achieves a set of key goals. Having all educators—teachers, administrators, and monitors and other support staff—learn the Five-Step Framework ensures that students can get help from the adult in school they most trust. In addition, having all educators familiar with an identical discussion outline allows a school to deliver a consistent response to targets no matter whom they choose for help and makes providing help efficient, easy to deliver, and repeatable. In short, the Five-Step Framework provides students with consistent support and control over next steps.

The Five-Step Framework to guide a support discussion consists of the following steps:

1. **listen:** the student talks about the problem while the adult listens carefully

2. **empathize:** the adult expresses understanding about how the student feels
3. **educate:** the adult explains what bullying is and how it works
4. **empower:** the adult and student discuss ways to respond to aggression to render it ineffective
5. **take action:** the adult and student develop a plan to get the bullying to stop

The key goals for the discussion are:

- **healing:** start the process of reversing the harm caused by bullying by helping the student understand that she is not flawed, the bullying is not personal, and that any perceived barriers to social/peer acceptance can be overcome (listen, empathize, and educate)
- **empowerment:** help the student understand how aggression works and how specific responses can eliminate the benefits to the aggressor so that the student learns effective responses to aggression (educate and empower)
- **action plan:** develop a plan for getting the bullying to stop, which involves either having the student try different responses to the aggression or having the adult engage administration to initiate Constructive Consequences (take action)

Although a support discussion involving five steps might seem to be a time-intensive effort, the reality is that most discussions will not proceed through all steps. Some students may just want someone to talk to (listen and empathize) so they feel valued and have their feelings validated. Some discussions may touch on responses to aggression (education), and then the student may decide to learn more on her own using the student guide (see chapter 10). Some students may simply want an adult to immediately intervene (take action). But since each step by itself can help students, discussions that do not cover all five are still beneficial. Discussions should not strictly adhere to the framework but should feel informal and natural; the adult should follow the student's lead. The framework simply helps the adult keep the discussion points and key goals in mind.

While healing, empowerment, and an action plan are key goals for the discussion, achieving them can take time. Reversing the harm requires that students see themselves and their relationship to their peers differently, which may take a few days, weeks, or even months. Following a discussion, students may need numerous rounds of social interactions with peers before they feel comfortable using newly learned responses to aggression. And it may take an aggressor time to recognize that a reliable "easy" target is now responding differently and that the aggression no longer provides social benefits.

Five-Step Framework: Details, Benefits, and Considerations

The following describes each step of the framework, the benefit each step delivers, and any special actions or considerations associated with each step.

Step 1: Listen

- **Primary action:** The adult lets the student talk about and describe the problem and her feelings. The adult should only interject or interrupt with clarifying questions. The adult should not ask for the names of the students involved.
- **Benefit:** The student feels better just by having someone know about the problem.
- **Special action—Assess risk:** At this step and at all other times during the discussion, the adult should listen carefully for any statement that suggests the student may be at risk of self-harm or harm to others. If a student makes a statement that explicitly or implicitly suggests that she is a danger to herself or others, the adult should discuss the statement with the student to assess the intent. A student may make such a statement simply to convey how badly she feels, not because she intends anyone harm. However, if the adult believes the student truly intends harm, the adult should discuss it with the student and let the student know that she may need additional help and support. As soon as the session concludes, the adult should document the discussion and notify administration.

Step 2: Empathize

- **Primary action:** The adult lets the student know that he understands how awful bullying can be and how the aggressor's actions make the student feel. Optionally, the adult can share a personal bullying story to let the student know that adults have also been through similar experiences.
- **Benefit:** The student feels valued and understood and takes comfort in having her feelings validated.
- **Special action—Assess need to continue:** The first two steps (listen and empathize) can deliver benefit to a student and in some cases may be as far as the student wishes to go in the discussion. The adult should explain that he can discuss why peers use aggression and ways that the student can get the bullying to stop. The adult should ask the student if she wishes to proceed to these topics. If not, the adult should let the student know that they can discuss those topics later if the student wishes.

Step 3: Educate

- **Primary action:** The adult explains bullying, specifically how aggression provides a social benefit and how the type of aggression that the student is facing, whether dominance, rejective, or relational, works to provide that benefit. The adult should point out that the aggressor likely directs similar aggression at others so the student knows that the bullying is not personal.
- **Benefit:** The student realizes that she is not flawed and that any characteristic explicitly or implicitly used in the bullying is not a barrier to peer acceptance. The student also realizes that she is not responsible for the bullying. In addition, understanding how aggression works and how it provides benefits lays the foundation for enabling the student to use effective responses.
- **Special action—Investigate possibility of underlying conflict:** The adult asks if there could be an underlying conflict with the aggressor that is driving the bullying, such as a fight or an argument, or if the aggressor may be offended by something the student did or said. Ask the student if she has apologized for anything recently or in the past and, if so, if she knew or specified what she was apologizing for. If conflict is suspected, review the empowerment techniques related to conflict resolution in chapter 10.

Step 4: Empower

- **Primary action:** The adult explains how reactions to aggression can make it more effective and how certain responses can render it ineffective. The adult and student discuss specifically how the student has reacted to the aggression and if there are better ways to respond.
- **Benefit:** The student understands how to thoughtfully respond to the aggression to render it ineffective. These responses are described and illustrated in the student guide and are described in chapter 10.
- **Special action—Role-play:** Some students may benefit from role-playing responses to aggression with the adult. The students should play both parts, the aggressor and target, to get the aggressor's perspective on the aggression and interaction.

Step 5: Take action

- **Primary action:** This step involves developing an action plan. The adult explains the options for getting the bullying to stop, including the Constructive Consequences and Chain of Custody Awareness mechanisms. The student can elect to try responses to the aggression or to have adults intervene. If the student elects to try responses first, the adult and student can agree to meet again if the responses are not working. If the student chooses adult intervention, the adult notifies administration. The student, however, still has a role to play even if administration is notified. The student should still try responses to the aggression if faced with it again and should report continued instances of aggression.

- **Benefit:** The student has a concrete plan to get the bullying to stop.
- **Special action—Reassure in cases of relational aggression:** In cases where relational aggression has damaged the student's friendships, the adult should let the student know that healing and friendship repair can take time. The adult should encourage her to build new relationships with peers outside her former social group. The adult should be very empathetic and should let her know she can always reach out again if she needs to talk.
- **Special action—Remind the student to be patient:** The adult should let the student know that responses to aggression can take time to work and may be difficult to do the first few times. Responses may not result in immediate success because it can take time for the aggressor to realize that the student's behavior has changed. The student should know that if the responses do not work, she can always have adults intervene.
- **Special action—Give the student responsibility:** If adult engagement is selected by the student, the student must still try to use effective responses to aggression. The student should also report instances of aggression to help the adults who are trying to resolve the problem.

No matter which option the student chooses, the student should know that she can reach out to the adult at any time for further help.

Rights and Responsibilities

The process for providing support must adhere to certain principles and guidelines in order to establish and maintain student trust. Students who engage adults for help with a bullying problem have the following rights:

- **student right to confidentiality:** no information about the discussion should be proactively shared with anyone unless the student requests adult intervention, the adult fears that the student poses a risk to herself or others, or a serious incident occurs (e.g., action on the part of the student in school or at home) that could be related to the bullying.
- **student right to withhold names:** the student should not be required to name the aggressor and any supporters unless the student requests adult intervention. An ideal outcome of the discussion is for the student to change how she responds to the aggression to render it ineffective, a solution that makes knowing the aggressor's name unnecessary. Students must be given the opportunity to handle the problem on their own if they wish, especially since they may be seeing the aggressor daily for years to come.

- **student right to choose between trying responses or adult intervention:** many students want to solve their bullying problem on their own. Unless an adult fears for the student's or others' safety or believes that the bullying must be stopped to prevent a serious incident, the student should be allowed to choose the course of action.

- **student right to opt out of parent notification:** parent notification can be extremely helpful to the problem resolution process in that parents can provide excellent support to their children. However, there may be a good reason why the student does not want his or her parents to know. For example, the parents may hold certain views about bullying that would make notification counterproductive. The student may also have already tried to get parent support but was unsuccessful. The educator should discuss parent notification with the student and provide the opportunity for the student to express any reluctance to such notification. If the student strongly objects and believes notification would be counterproductive, notification can be withheld or at least delayed. The exception to this rule is if the educator feels the student has been seriously harmed by the bullying or if there is a risk of self-harm or harm to others. In such cases the school should notify the parents.

The following are the adult rights and responsibilities:

- **adult right to intervene based on risk:** if a student implicitly or explicitly indicates a desire or intention to harm others and the adult believes the student may act, the adult will document what the student said and immediately notify administration.

- **adult responsibility to complete the support process:** a student who selects an adult to help with a bullying problem is putting faith in the adult that she is going to help solve the problem, whether by providing the student with skills that can stop the bullying or by intervening at the student's request. Adults selected by students who start the support process have a responsibility to follow through and complete the process.

- **adult limited right to notify parents:** an adult should notify a student's parents only after discussing it with the student first. Notification should be done if the student is in clear need of additional support and if parent involvement is needed to help stop aggression outside of school. The adult should, however, ensure the parents will not make the problem worse. Adult notification should include an overview of bullying so the parents understand the topic and can provide objective and effective support (see chapter 11).

- **adult responsibility not to act unilaterally:** one of the barriers to a student engaging an adult is fear of the adult taking unilateral action such as engaging the aggressor or notifying parents. Adults should discuss any actions that they feel are necessary with the student they are helping prior to taking that action.

Respecting student rights will help reassure students that they can trust adults to help.

Continuance and Transition

When a student elects to try getting the bullying to stop on her own, the adult should ask the student to report back on progress. If the student doesn't report back, the adult should follow up to get the status and take the following actions:

- If the student has not succeeded but is optimistic and still trying, the adult should provide encouragement and follow up again.
- If the student has succeeded, congratulations are in order for overcoming the problem.
- If the student has not succeeded and appears to be even more negatively affected, the adult should revisit the topic of having adults intervene.
- If a student engages an adult and starts a discussion but the adult is leaving the school community before the bullying problem is resolved, the adult should notify the student and ask if there is another adult the student would like to talk to. The adult should suggest another adult if necessary and have a conversation with this other adult summarizing the student's situation.

Removal of Barriers to Reporting

7

> **Overview:** Success at addressing bullying issues is dependent on creating an environment where targets are willing to report them. Since bullying issues cannot always be identified from student behavior, and targets are the only ones who can confirm that bullying is occurring, the school must create an environment where targets will proactively report bullying problems. To do this, schools must remove the common barriers to reporting.

Barriers to Reporting

Almost all schools have a formal process for reporting a bullying problem, such as an online form, that is often mandated by district policy. However, simply providing a means of reporting a bullying problem is not sufficient to be broadly effective since the mechanism alone doesn't remove barriers to reporting. The reporting process won't be used in all bullying cases until the barriers are removed.

Targets do not report bullying issues for a variety of reasons, including:

- **fear of wider awareness:** targets do not want others to know about the problem.
- **social cost:** related to wider awareness, targets fear the social cost they may incur if they report a bullying problem and peers find out. Peers of the target who are aware of the bullying may not report the problem for the same reason.
- **loss of control:** targets fear that by reporting a bullying problem, they will lose control over how the problem is handled, whether by educators or parents, and the outcome, which can result in the bullying getting worse and a social cost.
- **risk of retaliation:** related to loss of control, targets know that if adults impose a punitive consequence on the aggressor, the bullying may get worse.

- **erroneous belief that peer treatment is deserved:** some targets believe the peer rejection they experience is deserved and due to a personal flaw and do not recognize their situation as a bullying issue.
- **feeling of shame:** some targets feel ashamed by their inability to get unwanted aggression to stop and the need for adult help.
- **fear of dismissal:** targets may fear that adults won't understand, will dismiss their problem as unimportant or trivial, or won't show any empathy.
- **assumption that adults condone the behavior:** when bullying that students are aware of takes place in front of an educator and the educator does not intervene, the students may erroneously believe that adults condone the bullying, which also reinforces to the target that the aggression is deserved.
- **fear of parental notification:** some targets come from cultural backgrounds in which being the target of bullying is considered a weakness and fear that parent notification will result in a negative consequence at home.
- **reluctance to talk to the principal or designated administrator:** due to the personal nature of a bullying problem, some students may want to talk to a favorite teacher or other adult who may not be a member of the administration or guidance department.
- **fear that educators favor or will side with an aggressor who is popular:** students who are popular with peers may be popular with educators as well; some targets may believe that educators won't be objective in addressing their bullying problem and, like peers, will side the aggressor.

Actions to Remove Reporting Barriers

The following are actions that schools can take to encourage reporting:

- **explain school policy:** explain the Constructive Consequences mechanism to let all students know how bullying problems will be handled, specifically that punitive consequences are not initially applied, and any consequence that is applied is a result of aggressor action, not a target's report. In addition, mention that parents won't always be notified in bullying cases.
- **pledge confidentiality:** let students know that all conversations about a bullying problem are kept confidential.
- **pledge to work in partnership:** let students know that administrators will listen to target concerns and will not take action, such as initiating the Constructive Consequences mechanism, unless requested or approved by the target.
- **educate students:** provide comprehensive bullying education to students so they understand what it is and why it happens, and actions they can take on their own to get it to stop.

- **create a support network of adults:** let students know that they can talk to any adult in the school about the problem and adults will take the problem seriously.
- **periodically remind students of school policy and support options:** implement the Antibullying Announcement mechanism (described in chapter 8) to periodically remind students how bullying issues will be handled and how adults will provide support.

Importance of Control for Targets

Targets fear losing control over the actions that adults might take in trying to resolve a bullying problem. In addition, the ideal way for students to resolve a bullying problem is on their own. A target who learns how to respond to aggression to get it to stop and successfully does so gains confidence and self-esteem, earns back lost social status, and knows how to handle future aggression.

When a target reports a bullying problem, the educator engaged by the target should ask if the target would like to try to get the bullying to stop on her own or have the educator initiate Constructive Consequences. The educator can discuss the type of aggression involved and talk about the specific ways of responding to it that can render it ineffective. With educator encouragement (but not a directive!), the target may want to try stopping it herself. If a target tries and is not successful, or insists on adult intervention, then educators can intervene. Every bullying issue is an opportunity for target education and empowerment.

In some cases where a target does not want adult intervention, educators may view a bullying problem as serious enough to warrant immediate intervention. In these cases, educators should explain to the targets the concerns they have and why they believe they need to take immediate action. They should reassure the targets that they will maintain confidentiality and first use Constructive Consequences to get the bullying to stop.

Parental Notification

Educators need to make their own judgments about whether to adhere to the commitment to not immediately notify parents about a bullying issue. A student who is suffering significant harm could benefit from parental support. However, it may not be in the target's best interest to notify parents if they do not have an accurate understanding of bullying. Parents may blame their child for the bullying problem, may view the bullying as indicative of a weakness in their child, may push their child to take action that the child may not want to take, may minimize or dismiss the seriousness of the issue, may initiate an antagonistic engagement with administration, or may push for punishment of the aggressor, all actions that can make the problem worse. It is recommended that educators always notify parents in cases of significant harm or where there is fear of the target committing self-harm. In cases where targets want to try to get the bullying to stop on their own or where targets would like the Constructive Consequences mechanism to be initiated, educators should consider waiting before notifying the target's parents. If educators feel that parental notification is necessary, they should explain why and commit to helping the parents understand how the targets want to be helped and actions that can make the problem worse.

Student Trust and Method Fidelity

The mechanisms of this Method serve as a contract with the students that they can trust adults to take appropriate action. Educators who advertise the mechanisms of this Method to their student body but do not follow through on the actions specified by the mechanisms will break the trust of their students and will have an even harder time dealing with bullying problems. The degree to which educators adhere to the mechanisms with fidelity has a direct correlation on the willingness of targets to report bullying problems.

Antibullying Announcement 8

Overview: One tool to remove barriers to student reporting of bullying issues is the periodic Antibullying Announcement. This communication lets students know that educators do not condone bullying but need student help in identifying it and describes exactly how educators will deal with a bullying problem. Reminding students periodically of this ensures that students who may be newly involved in a bullying issue and may have ignored or "tuned out" a prior communication know how to get help.

Overcoming the Challenge of Bullying Issue Awareness

One reason that some bullied students do not ask for help is that they get the mistaken impression that adults in the school condone bullying behaviors when the adults witness the aggression but do not intervene. Students may not realize that adults simply cannot tell which of the aggressions they witness cause harm. In addition, students may assume that adults will take actions that will make the problem worse, and the students will pay a social price for requesting help.

One way to encourage students to ask for help is through the Antibullying Announcement. This periodic antibullying "public service announcement" is delivered on a regular basis to all students so that they know that adults do not condone bullying, that they can come to any adult for help, and that they can be confident that adults will not make the problem worse. Key parts of the Antibullying Announcement are an admission by educators that they cannot always identify bullying based on observed behaviors and a request for student help to know when bullying is occurring.

The Antibullying Announcement

The Antibullying Announcement is delivered by an educator and includes the following:

- a statement that adults do not condone behaviors that cause others to feel hurt, scared, rejected, flawed, or excluded (i.e., bullying)

- an admission that adults cannot always identify behaviors that cause harm from all the student interactions that they observe
- a request for help from the students in identifying bullying problems
- an offer on behalf of all adults in the school to provide help with a bullying problem; students can ask any adult they choose, not just the principal or the adult making the Antibullying Announcement, and the conversation will be confidential
- an explanation of what adults will do to help a student who comes forward, including that the adult and student will discuss the problem and talk about a variety of solutions, the adult will not take action unless the student agrees, and an explanation of what that action would be, specifically the Constructive Consequences and Chain of Custody Awareness mechanisms
- a pledge that adults will try not to make the problem worse or take action that the student asking for help does not want, such as unilaterally engaging the aggressor or notifying parents

As a result of the Antibullying Announcement, students will know that they can report bullying problems—their own and their peers'—without fear of retaliation, paying a social price, or losing control of the resolution process. They know that adults will maintain their confidence and work with them in partnership on solutions, and they have a clear understanding of the constructive actions that adults will take when they become aware of a bullying problem. Students will view adults in their school as trusted and reliable resources who can help with bullying problems.

Delivery

The Antibullying Announcement should be delivered by the educator who is closest to the students. Classroom teachers are ideal, particularly homeroom teachers or those who are with a particular group of students most often during the day. The educator must emphasize that any adult in the school can help in case a target does not feel comfortable engaging with the educator making the Announcement.

Frequency

The Antibullying Announcement should be made regularly, such as once every month or two, since bullying issues arise periodically. The students who will pay the most attention are those who are targets at the time the Announcement is made. Those not involved in a bullying issue may simply ignore the Announcement. Periodic delivery ensures that students who need the information most get it.

Preconditions

Schools should not start making the Antibullying Announcement until the other mechanisms of the Method have been implemented. The Antibullying Announcement essentially asks students to take a leap of faith that adults know how to help the right way and will not let them down. Starting the Antibullying Announcement while traditional mechanisms are in place or before educators have practiced and are comfortable with this Method's mechanisms could potentially do more harm than good by breaking student trust and damaging educator credibility.

Warning!

When educators make the first Antibullying Announcement, they should be prepared for a significant number of students coming forward and asking for help. The initial response may be overwhelming. The explanation of why bullying behaviors are occurring, why adults were seemingly doing nothing to stop them, and how adults can help without making the problem worse may bring such a sense of relief to some students that they may burst into tears. Educators may have the wonderful problem of needing to provide support to a significant number of students given that at any one time in a typical school, up to 20% of students are suffering harm from aggression. Educators must be prepared to provide the support they advertise through the Antibullying Announcement.

The good news, beyond surfacing and addressing all the bullying issues, is that over time, with sustained practice of the Method's mechanisms, students will come forward when issues arise rather than all at once when an Antibullying Announcement is made. Further, with sustained practice of and fidelity to the Method's mechanisms, the overall number of bullying issues in the school should decrease over time.

Classroom Strategies

9

> **Overview:** Classroom Strategies describe actions that teachers can take to influence positive changes in behavior at the individual, peer group, and whole-class levels. The actions are grouped into two categories, "Positive Cultural Changes" and "Direct Interventions." Cultural changes can be implemented at any time and indirectly help to prevent and reduce bullying. Direct interventions are proactive in terms of preventing bullying and reactive to bullying issues.

The Opportunity to Influence

Classroom teachers occupy a unique position in bullying prevention efforts in that they best know their students' social structures and dynamics. This knowledge provides teachers with an opportunity to influence student behavior and resolve specific bullying problems through a variety of actions that can change the cultural environment and exert influence over the behavior of individuals and peer groups. Most importantly, teachers can identify the chronically targeted students who occupy the lowest positions on the social hierarchy and support them by helping to expand their social networks and directly stopping bullying.

Positive Cultural Changes

Make the Antibullying Announcement Monthly or Bimonthly

Teachers should periodically reiterate that adults do not condone bullying, ask for help in identifying bullying, and review how bullying problems will be addressed. Not only does this help to surface bullying problems, but it lets all students know that the teacher is aware of their behavior and not ignoring it.

Make Social Changes to Reduce Bullying

Although teachers may have limited direct influence over student friendships and an individual's popularity among peers, they can influence the social environment. Teachers can determine where students sit and who they work with on projects. They can also encourage individuals to take part in certain social activities. Teachers can indirectly foster friendships among students, especially between students who belong to different social groups. Such opportunities can include the following:

- conducting team-building exercises where popular and less popular individuals are paired on a team, which may help blur group boundaries and provide less popular individuals with a status boost
- asking a popular student to show a new student around, which may give the new student an enhanced level of acceptance
- encouraging a target or less popular student to participate in activities, e.g., extracurricular, that may help increase the target's social network
- asking a former student who has moved to a higher grade to be a "buddy" to a current student who may have a minimal social network; the buddy actions can be as simple as saying hello to the student in the hallways, on the playground, and in the cafeteria
- separating group members, particularly where a group's leader may use aggression to maintain her role, or where the group maintains its identity primarily through the use of aggression directed at lower-status students
- arranging seating in configurations that separate peer group leaders from members and from targets to reduce aggression

Any creative actions that modify social structures to reduce aggression, "flatten" the social hierarchy, and help the least popular students broaden their social network can benefit the overall goal of bullying prevention.

Please note that teachers should not try to address or fix a bullying issue by pairing an aggressor and a target. In cases where a target has been harmed by the aggressor, the target often just wants the aggression to stop and a separation from the aggressor, not to be forced to spend more time with the aggressor. Any repair of a relationship between an aggressor and target needs to occur organically and through a sincere effort on the part of the aggressor in order for the repair to provide a benefit to the target.

Self-Assess and Model Respect

Students in a class, particularly where they have a good relationship with the teacher and are eager for the teacher's approval, will take cues on how to treat peers from how the teacher treats peers. If a teacher treats a student differently from others for whatever reason, even through the use of subtle body language or tone of voice, the students may also treat that student differently in order to gain the teacher's approval. Teachers must be aware of how they treat each student and ensure they don't express personal negative feelings through words or actions toward individual students.

Avoid Teaching Contempt

Contempt for a characteristic, whether of the body, race, religion, disability, gender identity, sports team affiliation, political leaning, socioeconomic status, etc., is taught. Children don't naturally develop feelings of contempt. Contempt is a reflection of the feelings and attitudes of one or more adults in the child's life. Contempt is dehumanizing. A student who feels contempt for a characteristic is more likely to direct aggression toward a person with that characteristic and will consider the behavior justified, no matter how much harm is being caused. Teachers should be careful to avoid expressions of contempt, even innocuous-seeming examples such as toward fans of a rival sports team.

Direct Interventions

Identify and Help Chronically Targeted Students

Perhaps the single most important action a teacher can take is to identify and help any chronically targeted students in the class. These are the students who occupy the lowest social position and are frequently the targets of aggression by the rest of the class. These individuals are "safe" for everyone to target since they generally have little peer support and there is no risk of becoming their target. In groups of students that have been together for a long period of time, e.g., multiple grades, these students may have been targets for an extended period (i.e., years) and the treatment by the class has become normalized. The students in the class won't view their treatment of that peer as anything out of the ordinary.

Teachers should proactively identify these chronically targeted students, discreetly determine if they are being harmed by the aggression, and, if so, provide help. Teachers can provide support using the Five-Step Framework. Helping these students also requires helping peers to recognize the harm they are causing. Persistent intervention by the teacher in terms of stopping aggression can help make students recognize their aggression as inappropriate and reverse the normalization of the behavior that has occurred over time.

Monitor Students with Obvious Differences

Students who have physical or behavioral characteristics that are markedly different from their peers, such as a disability or a difference in average height and/or weight, manner of speech, dress, skin color, ethnicity, etc., are more likely to be targets of aggression. Teachers who have students with a markedly different characteristic should watch for aggression directed at these students and intervene when the aggression involves an implicit reference to the characteristic.

Influence Peer Groups

Since friends within a peer group usually share similar views on bullying, educators, particularly those viewed as mentors by one or more members of the group, can influence the entire peer group by getting one student to change behavior. Mentors can be particularly helpful when educators identify an aggressor who is bullying a target. The mentor can use the student's desire for the mentor's approval to help get the aggression to stop by expressing disapproval of the behavior and faith in the student's ability to change the behavior.

Influence Popular Students

Since popular students determine the level of acceptance of aggression within a class, teachers who have good relationships with these students, particularly where the students value the teacher's approval, can influence these students to reject aggression in order to make it less accepted by the class. As aggression tends to "flow down" the social hierarchy, getting those at the top to change behavior and frown upon those who use certain aggressions, such as aggressions that use a personal characteristic, can reduce harmful aggression in the entire peer group.

Activate Bystanders

Bystanders have the power to stop bullying incidents and make aggression less accepted by peers. Activating bystanders can deliver significant positive change. Activating bystanders means that the teacher talks directly (discreetly and privately) with individual students or small groups of students to encourage action.

Those bystanders who simply observe often do not like what they see but they do not know if they should intervene or how to intervene. Higher-status students should be encouraged to defend targets using indirect intervention techniques. These techniques are described in chapter 10 and in the student guide. Popular students have a greater chance of success than less popular students in getting bullying to stop without risk to status or of becoming a target.

Teachers can also encourage students to support those who intervene. Students are reluctant to intervene due to the risk of incurring a social cost. Students who support or express approval for those who do intervene provide a social benefit and reinforce the behavior. Students can support defenders of targets either verbally or through positive body language and either while the intervention is occurring or after the fact.

Teachers should acknowledge to students in all cases that taking action is difficult and emphasize that students should only take action if they are comfortable doing so. Teachers should never ask students to directly intervene given the risks to social status and of becoming a bullying target. And given the risks that intervention carries, teachers should never judge or express displeasure with students who are encouraged to act but do not.

Discourage Supporters

Some students may show support for aggressors. The supporters may be friends of the aggressor or may be students who wish to curry favor with the aggressor and her friends in order to get a boost in social status. Teachers can talk with supporters individually to let them know that supporting aggression also causes harm to the target and makes a person subject to the discipline process. If the supporter is merely showing approval for the aggression but not directly joining in, suggest that he turn away from the bullying so as not to provide implicit encouragement or approval.

Create a Social Map

Social structures transfer from one school year to the next where class compositions are maintained. Teachers can help both their colleagues and the students by sharing information on these social structures, particularly by identifying individuals who are chronic targets of aggression. The idea is not to prejudice the new teacher against any of the students but to start the new school year with an immediate awareness of social structures and any historically problematic peer-to-peer interactions that may continue.

Student Education and Empowerment

Overview: Teaching students how aggression works to positively affect social status and how to respond to it to reduce or eliminate the benefits can allow them to address issues on their own and avoid harm. Further, this education can help boost student self-esteem and enable students to successfully navigate challenging relationships, a skill that provides a lifetime of benefits. Student understanding of bullying can also help lead to cultural change where aggression as a means of boosting social status becomes less accepted. The more effective students are at resolving bullying issues on their own, the less time adults will have to spend addressing them.

Education and Empowerment Scope

Student Education and Empowerment results in all students understanding what bullying is, how it works, why it occurs, and ways that they can respond to it, both as a target and a bystander, to get it to stop. Students learn how to avoid reacting to aggression in ways that can make it more effective and instead to thoughtfully respond to it in a way that makes it ineffective or less effective at providing social benefits (target empowerment). They also learn how to help bullied peers using methods that reduce or eliminate risk of becoming targets (bystander intervention). Students who are not able to resolve a bullying problem on their own learn how to work with an adult to get the bullying to stop without risk of retaliation or of the problem becoming worse.

Student Guide and Implementation

All students in grades 3–8 are provided with a bullying education guide that was developed for use with this Method. *What YOU Can Do About Bullying by Max and Zoey* is a graphic comic–style guide that covers bullying basics, bystander intervention, empowerment techniques, how to get bullying to stop, and ways to engage an adult.

The student guide is intended to be read in private, ideally at home. It can also be used as a social emotional learning supplement, to be read individually or in a group. Because targets don't want others to know that they have a bullying problem, having a few copies available for students in a public place, such as a classroom or library, may prevent students who need the information from accessing it.

Other books and materials can certainly be used for student education in addition to the Method's student guide; however, educators should ensure that the content is aligned with the principles of this Method.

Student Guide Contents

The student guide describes the same information in the adult education component though written at the student level and with illustrations. The student guide contains the following sections:

- **Good Things to Know:** teaches a few friendship basics such as learning the right way to apologize, creating a circle of friends, how one person in a three-person group may be excluded, how everyone has unique characteristics, and what to do about name-calling
- **Learn the Bullying Basics:** introduces key terms and explains what bullying is and why students do it
- **Bullyproof Yourself:** describes ways of thoughtfully responding to aggression to render it ineffective at providing a social benefit, and proactive actions to prevent relational aggression from starting
- **How to Help a Bullied Person:** explains bystander intervention techniques including indirect ways of intervening as a bystander, direct intervention in physical and verbal bullying, and how to stop relational aggression
- **If You Are Being Bullied:** provides encouragement in trying responses to aggression to get it to stop and suggests enlisting the help of a trusted adult if needed
- **Train Your Adult Helper:** intended for the target to share with an adult, the section explains the wrong and right ways to help a target for the benefit of both the target and the adult

Target Empowerment

The student guide empowers targets by teaching them ways to thoughtfully respond to aggression to reduce or eliminate the social benefits to the aggressor. Responses to dominance and rejective aggression can also decrease the likelihood that it will be repeated. Relational aggression, however, requires prevention to keep it from starting; immediate and sustained counteraction to stop or limit the damage if it does start; and an understanding and acceptance of certain outcomes if the aggression succeeds. The sections below describe the target empowerment actions listed and illustrated in the student guide. These actions can also be suggested by educators to targets during the education step of the Five-Step Framework.

Basic Principles of Empowerment

In dominance aggression, aggressors use threats and intimidation to instill fear in a target. When a target shows fear, it communicates to observing peers that the aggressor is someone to be feared. This can allow the aggressor to earn the respect of bystanders. Conversely, if an aggressor attempts to intimidate a person who is unaffected or amused, the aggressor fails to gain respect from those watching and may even lose respect and social status.

In rejective aggression, aggressors use insults, mocking, or antagonism to appear clever and entertaining to observing peers, to reinforce the identity of a peer group, or to associate with and gain the approval of a group of higher-status peers. The way the target reacts to the aggression can enhance the social benefit. For example, when an insult makes everyone laugh, the aggressor may gain peer approval and social status. If the target gets upset, the aggression may be even more entertaining to observing peers, increasing the social benefit enjoyed by the aggressor. But if the target joins in and laughs or responds in a way that makes what the aggressor said seem not funny, the aggressor may not gain and can even lose status.

In relational aggression, aggressors attempt to damage the target's friendships. The aggressor starts a campaign to rally others to her side and to socially isolate the target. If successful, the aggressor maintains a circle of friends while the target winds up alone. A target who takes no action when faced with a relational aggression campaign frequently winds up isolated. A target who talks to the aggressor or a participant and tries to stop the campaign may succeed in retaining friends, preventing the loss of status. A failed campaign may even reduce the aggressor's status.

Responses to Dominance Aggression

Responses to dominance aggression generally require a target to resist a natural or instinctive feeling of fear of harm and rely on an understanding of how this aggression is used by the aggressor to appear dominant to observing peers. Responses that demonstrate a lack of fear while not insulting or making the aggressor appear foolish are important because they allow an aggressor to stop the behavior without a social cost.

Show no fear. In dominance aggression, aggressors try to instill fear of physical harm in their targets. Expressing fear, such as shrinking back, cowering, and trying to get away, is what earns the aggressor respect from observing peers. A target who stops showing fear, even if just an act, shows those watching that the aggressor is not someone to be feared. The aggressor will fail to gain respect from others and may even lose some respect.

Talk. In dominance aggression, a target who talks to the aggressor may be able to get the aggression to stop. Silence can be an indication of fear; however, talking demonstrates that a target is not afraid. Further, a target who establishes a personal relationship with an aggressor may be less likely to be targeted; an aggressor may find the relationship with the target to be more of a social benefit than the benefit gained by intimidating the target. Targets who are gracious and complimentary are also more difficult to intimidate as it makes the aggressor look bad in the eyes of observing peers. Talking can also surface an underlying reason for the conflict, such as offense, that the target and aggressor can then resolve.

Say "no" as though to a friend. Dominance aggression may sometimes involve an aggressor making a demand of the target, such as handing over money or a personal item. The demand is made not so much to get what is asked for, but to demonstrate to observing peers that the target won't dare refuse. The intimidating way the aggressor makes the demand implies that a refusal will be met with physical harm. In this situation, the target can say "no" to the aggressor but in the same way he would to a friend. The target can say, "I'd love to, but I can't" or "I wish I could, but I can't" and then give a plausible reason why. This type of response can change the dynamic of the situation in two ways. First, the target is showing no fear by talking with the aggressor and expressing a desire to help. Second, the target's response puts the aggressor in a position of either trying to force the target to comply, which may be frowned upon by observing peers and reduce the aggressor's status, or saving face by accepting the target's explanation. Saying "no" in a way that puts the target on the same side as the aggressor makes it harder for the aggressor to fault the target for the answer.

Don't respond with physical aggression. A person who is subjected to physical aggression such as pushes and shoves has every right to defend himself to prevent injury but should not fight back. Fighting back could result in serious injury. Further, a person who appears unaffected by physical aggression appears unintimidated to those watching.

Apply the "friend test." A target who experiences physical aggression may be tempted to immediately tell an adult. However, before that step is taken, the target should ask what he would do if a friend did the same thing. If the target wouldn't tell an adult if the friend had made similar physical contact, he should think carefully about telling an adult. Sometimes an aggressor who uses light physical contact wants the target to tell an adult since it can make the target look "weak" in front of peers. And telling an adult confirms that the aggressor made the target upset. Further, the aggressor may feel confident that the physical contact is minor enough that it won't result in a consequence, which may make the target even more upset. A target subjected to physical contact should try to respond in the way he would if a friend had done the same thing. But if the contact goes beyond what might be expected from a friend horsing around or is hurtful, and the target wants the behavior to stop immediately, the target should engage an adult for help.

Responses to Rejective Aggression

Responses to rejective aggression will not always eliminate the social benefit, but they can minimize the benefit and prevent the behaviors from being repeated. Aggression intended to make the aggressor appear clever or entertaining can be easiest to render ineffective because the target's reaction plays a role in providing a benefit. Aggression that focuses on a characteristic of a target for the purpose of reinforcing a group's bonds or identity may be less affected by responses, though they can still be helpful.

Don't get upset. In some types of rejective aggression, the aggressor's goal is to entertain observing peers. That goal is more likely to be met if the target gets upset, which can be more entertaining for observers. But if the target doesn't get upset, those watching may not be entertained or entertained as much, which can reduce or eliminate the social benefit to the aggressor.

Do the unexpected. In some instances of rejective aggression, aggressors expect the target to get upset in order to entertain others. But a target who does something unexpected, such as agreeing with the aggressor or taking an insult very seriously and pledging to do something about it, can take the spotlight off the aggressor and cause the target to be the one who gains a social benefit from observing peers. This will deprive the aggressor of satisfaction and increases the chances the aggression will stop.

Learn to laugh at oneself. In rejective aggression, aggressors may mention something embarrassing the target has done, post embarrassing photos or videos, or point out a unique characteristic of the target that others find funny in order to upset the target. However, if the target agrees with and laughs along with the aggressor, the social benefit to the aggressor is reduced or eliminated. The aggressor may try again, so the target has to persevere and keep laughing in order to get the aggressor to stop. Being able to laugh at oneself is a sign of self-confidence, a characteristic that can prevent aggression.

Own it; don't deny it. In rejective aggression, an aggressor who brings up something embarrassing about the target expects the target to deny it and get upset. A target who instead embraces and owns up to whatever the aggressor mentions or shares with peers denies the aggressor the attention that comes with being the source of the embarrassment. A target may still endure some amount of mocking and teasing by peers; however, the duration will be much shorter if the target owns up to the embarrassing action or situation.

Don't respond in kind. A target of rejective aggression may want to respond using the same type of aggression. A target being insulted or mocked might think to respond with an insult. This type of response might make those watching think that the target is upset, which benefits the aggressor. Using an aggressive response, particularly on social media where information can be shared widely and go viral, could also escalate the aggression. And an escalation of face-to-face aggression could lead to a physical altercation. A target shouldn't respond to aggression with the same behavior but should acknowledge it and respond in a nonaggressive way.

Actions That Prevent Relational Aggression

Relational aggression often starts without the target's awareness. The campaigns launched by aggressors use covert methods such as direct lobbying or pressuring of the target's friends, and rumors and passive aggression such as exclusion. The aggression can result in damaged friendships before the target is fully aware that it is happening. Once the aggression starts and spreads, it can be very difficult to resolve it in a way that restores the original friendships. For this reason, students should actively try to prevent relational aggression from starting by changing their daily social interactions in the ways listed below.

Express anger. Some people don't express their anger out of fear of having the anger dismissed or of losing the friend. The person may drop hints about the hurt or anger, such as being distant in the hope that the offender will ask what is wrong or will suffer from the person being distant. Or the person may take covert action to "get back" at the offender. Students need to know that every person has a right to express anger, and directly addressing an offense is the best way to resolve it and can make a friendship stronger.

Express anger the right way. The fear of losing a friend or of having feelings dismissed when expressing anger can be avoided if the student expresses anger the right way. The student should start with an affirmation of the friendship before mentioning the offending action. For example, the student can say, "You are my good friend, and your friendship means so much to me. However, we need to talk about something that hurt my feelings (or made me very angry)." And the student should always tell the reason for the anger. Telling the reason allows the offender to know what caused the conflict and to apologize for it.

Listen when someone is angry and own up to actions. When an offender is confronted by the anger of the offended person, a common reaction is for the offender to get defensive. No one likes to be accused, and sometimes the offender doesn't think that the action that made the person angry is a big deal. But if the action made the person angry, it is a big deal to that person. The offender should listen to what that person has to say, acknowledge the person's right to be angry, own up to any actions that contributed to the anger, and apologize.

Never apologize by just saying "sorry"; use the four-part apology. When a person is angry with a friend but doesn't say why and is distant, the loss of connection that the friend feels may become unbearable. So the friend, without knowing what she did wrong, may say "I'm sorry" just to make the friendship feel right again. However, just saying "sorry" does not resolve the underlying conflict. Only by apologizing for the action that caused the conflict can it be resolved. Once the reason for the conflict is known, the offender should use the four-part apology:

1. a statement of sorrow or regret, i.e., "I'm sorry . . ."
2. a statement of the action that caused the anger or hurt feelings

3. an acknowledgment of the other person's right to feel hurt or angry
4. a commitment to never again repeat the action that caused the hurt or anger

Although it can take time and effort, a friend should always find out the reason why the person is angry. Apologizing *for* something resolves the conflict. Apologizing without knowing why just postpones the conflict to a later date.

Practice expressing anger and apologizing. A great way to help prevent relational aggression is for friends to practice expressing anger and apologizing. Talking face-to-face with someone who is angry is difficult, which is one reason why people try to avoid it. Practicing before a person actually gets angry helps make both the person who is angry and the person apologizing more comfortable when the anger is real.

When practicing, the person playing the role of the offended person first reaffirms the value of the friendship and expresses the desire to remain friends, then expresses the hurt and anger over the friend's action. The person playing the role of the offender acknowledges the action, apologizes for it, acknowledges the friend's right to be angry, and commits to never doing the action again. Friends should take turns playing the role of the offender and offended.

Note that practicing expressing anger and apologies may bring up a real conflict that has been suppressed. The two people who intended just to practice apologizing now have a chance to resolve a real conflict and make their friendship stronger. The individuals should take a deep breath and follow the steps. When they are finished, they may likely be better friends than before.

Accept an apology and move on. Sometimes an apology does not make a person feel better. But if the friend was sincere in the apology, the person should accept that the friend is sorry and believe in her again. The hurt will fade in time, and the friendship will be even stronger.

Be honest and direct when breaking off a friendship. There is an easy wrong way and a hard right way to change friends. The easy wrong way is to use relational aggression, such as betrayal, to hurt the old friend so she won't want to be friends anymore. This approach allows the person to avoid guilt because the old friend is the one who ultimately breaks off the friendship. But this approach is not fair to the old friend, and the relational aggression may result in multiple lost friendships. The hard right way is for the person to tell the old friend face-to-face that while they've been great friends and have had a lot of fun together, the person no longer wants to be close friends.

Develop a circle of friends. While having just one best friend can feel good, a person may immediately feel isolated whenever conflict with that best friend arises. This can also compel a person to immediately apologize without knowing the reason for the conflict so as to preserve the friendship. Having many friends reduces the risk of harm and isolation from relational aggression.

Make a friendship pact. Friends should formally affirm to each other the value of the friendships and make a commitment to each other to bring up problems face-to-face, to listen when someone brings up a problem, to not gang up on one person, to be honest and respectful to each other, to never lie or betray or use relational aggression, and to help each other if one person becomes the target of aggression.

Accept only authentic friendship as the standard, nothing less. Authentic friendships are based on mutual respect, honesty, and caring. They allow individuals to be themselves and to be in touch with their feelings. Inauthentic and abusive friendships may feel authentic at times, but they are marked by periods of disrespect, dishonesty, and a lack of true caring. They can be characterized by manipulation, give individuals feelings of insecurity, and can make individuals not sure about who they are. People should accept only authentic friendship.

Never pay a price for friendship. Authentic friendships never come with a price. An authentic friend never asks a person to do something that the person doesn't want to do or knows isn't right. And if someone says that the person can be a friend if the person does something that isn't right, is unsafe, or may be illegal, the person should not accept the friendship. A true friend does not ask a person to prove her worth.

Never post online, send an email, or text when angry. It is very easy for an angry person to say things that she doesn't mean and will regret. In a private face-to-face conversation, unintended words spoken in anger are heard by one person, can be apologized for later, and are often quickly forgotten. In a private face-to-face conversation, unfair or inappropriate words said in anger are only heard by the other person, not by everyone, which makes an apology for those words easier for the person to accept. And facial expressions and body language can help limit what is said face-to-face.

Expressing anger in written form does not provide the same benefits and limiters of face-to-face conversation. A person may express things that she wouldn't otherwise have said in a face-to-face conversation. In addition, an electronic communication, such as an email, text, or online post, becomes a permanent record that can be shared to a limitless number of people. Even though the person might regret posted or emailed words, and although the person can apologize to the offended person, those words will always exist somewhere and may be known to a large audience. Sometimes words expressed in anger are so hurtful when known by others that the offended person may not be able to forgive them. So never email, text, post online, or make any kind of written electronic communication when angry.

Avoid embarrassing pictures and videos that the world shouldn't see. Embarrassing pictures and videos can appear online at the push of a button. And while a friend may promise to keep a picture or video secret forever, conflicts arise and friendships do end. Online images, however, can persist forever. A person should never allow themselves to be the subject of embarrassing pictures or videos that she would not want to appear online or have others see.

Responses That Counteract Relational Aggression

Counteracting relational aggression is challenging since the aggressor often uses covert actions. Targets of relational aggression must act quickly to identify the aggressor, the reason for the aggression, and contain and reverse any damage to friendships. The general rule is that if relational aggression is suspected, the target *must* take action.

A person who suddenly finds friends acting strangely or differently should assume that a covert relational aggression campaign has started. A common reaction is for the target to pretend it isn't happening. The reaction is understandable as friends may be sending mixed messages by acting friendly one moment but like a stranger the next. Inaction, however, causes a campaign to be successful. If friends are suddenly acting distant for no apparent reason, the target should assume that a relational aggression campaign has started. The target should not ignore the behavior or hope it will pass.

Identify and talk to the aggressor. A target of a relational aggression campaign must identify the aggressor and ask why the person is using the aggression. This may be very hard for targets to do as they may fear that acknowledging the campaign or confronting the aggressor will make the problem worse. Further, the target may fear that the aggressor will pretend not to know what the target is talking about. But talking directly to the aggressor can surface the issue that led to the campaign. If the aggression started due to a conflict, the target can try to resolve it and ask the aggressor to help reverse any damage from the campaign. If the aggression started because the aggressor views the target as a social threat, the target can try to put the aggressor at ease.

Enlist the help of friends and participants. If a target is unable to resolve the conflict with the aggressor, or the aggressor denies starting the campaign, won't talk to the target, or is unwilling to stop the campaign, the target should enlist the help of friends or campaign participants. Campaigns require participants to be successful. A target can ask friends to remain friends and not to support the campaign. This is also challenging as the target is essentially asking the participant to side with the target against both the aggressor and any participants who have already sided with the aggressor.

Don't retaliate. A target who is unable to get a campaign to stop may be tempted to launch a campaign against the aggressor. But the target should not retaliate. Two competing campaigns can get completely out of hand with disastrous results for both the aggressor and target.

Avoid participating in someone else's campaign. A person who is being pulled into a campaign should resist. Relational aggression requires the participation, knowingly or unknowingly, of others. Simply participating—by passing along a rumor, signing a petition, or agreeing not to be friends with someone—makes it effective. If someone asks a person to exclude someone or to stop being friends with someone, that person should realize that the request is an attempt at manipulation into campaign participation. An alternative to joining in is to determine if there is a conflict between the aggressor and the target and encourage the aggressor to resolve the conflict directly.

Accepting the Outcome of a Successful Relational Aggression Campaign

A successful relational aggression campaign leaves the target with damaged friendships, social isolation, and feelings of devastation. The target needs to know, however, that given enough time, life will get better. The target may be able to repair friendships and will make new friends. In the meantime, the target needs to accept the situation as acceptance allows for healing.

Bystander Empowerment

Peers who observe aggression (bystanders) can directly intervene to stop it. In dominance and rejective aggression, the bystander can disrupt the interaction between the aggressor and target or, more strongly, take the side of the target against the aggressor. In relational aggression, a bystander can refuse to participate in the campaign and can work to disrupt the campaign by alerting other members of the peer group about it and asking them not to participate.

Due to the risks that direct intervention carry, all students should be aware of ways that they can intervene indirectly. Indirect intervention allows the bystander to help the target without explicitly taking a stand against the aggressor. Indirect intervention includes disrupting interactions involving dominance and rejective aggression without taking a side, privately asking the aggressor to stop, and remaining neutral in relational aggression campaigns. Indirect intervention also includes providing support to the target through friendship and inclusion.

Indirect Intervention in Dominance and Rejective Aggression

A bystander can stop a dominance or rejective bullying episode without directly challenging the aggressor in several ways. The bystander can do the following:

- pretend to be unaware that bullying is occurring and disrupt it or make up an excuse to get the target away from the aggressor
- step into the interaction between the aggressor and target and simply suggest, without apparent judgment, that they all do some other activity
- talk to the target afterward to let the target know that the aggressor's behavior was not justified and that any characteristic used in the aggression is simply a characteristic, not a flaw; to empathize with the target about the pain caused by the aggression and the desire for the behavior to stop; and to let the target know that he has a friend or at least someone who cares and recognizes how he is being harmed

- talk to the aggressor and any supporters individually to express that the aggression was not right
- ask the aggressor in private if the behavior is conflict driven, and if so, encourage resolution of the conflict

Indirect Intervention in Relational Aggression

A bystander can stop a relational aggression campaign without directly challenging the aggressor in several ways. The bystander can do the following:

- simply not participate in the activity that harms the target; the bystander does not publicly declare opposition to the campaign but also does not take action to help the campaign succeed
- claim to be on the side of the aggressor but then remain neutral
- tell friends about the campaign and suggest that they don't participate. Refusal to participate or neutrality does carry some risk to social status if it is obvious to the aggressor and other campaign participants.
- make the target aware of the existence of the campaign and identity of the aggressor so the target has an opportunity to take action to stop the campaign and reverse any damage to friendships
- simply be a friend to the target to let her know that she is not alone. Talking to the target about the bullying can let her know that she has a friend or at least someone who cares and who recognizes how she is being harmed.
- talk in private with the aggressor to ask if the bullying was conflict driven and encourage resolution of the conflict
- encourage participants to restore relationships with the target

Guidance on Getting Help from an Adult

To address the fear that many students have about an adult making a bullying problem worse, the student guide has a section for adults to read on the wrong and right ways to help a bullied student. The target who asks an adult for help can show the adult this section of the guide and they can review it together. The wrong ways to respond include ignoring the student, dismissing the problem as unimportant, saying the wrong things, blaming the target for the bullying, giving unhelpful advice such as ignoring the aggressor, and taking action without the approval of the target. The right ways to respond mirror the Five-Step Framework and include listening, empathizing, educating, and working in partnership to solve the issue.

Parent Education and Engagement

11

> **Overview:** Some bullying issues may require the support of parents for resolution. In order for parents to be effective partners, they need to have an accurate understanding of the problem. Parents who have been educated on bullying are going to be better able to provide support for their children whether they are targets or aggressors. These parents will also be stronger partners in working with educators to resolve the problem. The language used when parents are engaged by educators for support can have an effect on the quality of the partnership. Educators should be mindful of the terms used and should ensure parents have a clear understanding of the mechanisms the school is using to address bullying issues.

Parent Education Resource

The CirclePoint website (www.circlepointbullying.com) has information specifically for parents about bullying, supporting a child involved in bullying, and working with educators in partnership to resolve a bullying problem. This information is found on the website's parent page. Educators can direct parents to the website either individually as the need arises or with a general communication about the school's adoption of the Method.

Parent Engagement

Parents can be critical partners in resolving a bullying problem, particularly where social media is involved. Educators may be challenged, however, by parents who do not accurately understand bullying. These parents may have preconceived notions or may have had bullying experiences or come from a cultural background that affects their perspective.

The language used in a discussion can also have an effect on how well parents partner with educators. Objective and concrete terms can reduce feelings of anger, a misplaced desire for justice, and defensiveness and can help forge a partnership and cooperation in resolving the problem. Educators need to keep in mind that bullying problems become easier to resolve when they are positioned as "behavioral change processes" and not judgments about individuals and their behaviors.

Language Guidelines

When discussing bullying with a parent, an educator should consider these guidelines around language:

- **Where possible, avoid using the terms "bully" and "bullying" due to their negative connotations.** Parents who are told their child is "bullying another" may become defensive and antagonistic toward educators and want to shield their child from these "accusations." Some parents may become angry with their child, mistakenly understanding "bullying" to mean intentional harm. Parents who are told that their child is "being bullied" will want to protect their child. They may blame the school for the problem and may demand justice. In addition, these terms have different meanings in various cultures. To some parents of certain ethnicities or nationalities, the terms can be a significant indictment of the child, whether the child is the aggressor or the target.
- **The term "bully" should never be used to describe an individual.** "Bully" is a dehumanizing label that implies that an individual only uses harmful aggression in social interactions. Being labeled a bully for behavior that is not intended to cause harm may be perceived as unfair and a slight.
- **Avoid using the term "aggressor."** Although "aggressor" is the term used to describe the student whose behavior is causing harm to the target, this term should be avoided when engaging with an aggressor and his or her parents. Instead, educators should refer to the specific behaviors used by the student.
- **Avoid using the term "target."** Although "target" is the term used to describe the student being harmed, it is not necessary to use it when dealing with a target and his or her parents. Instead, educators should refer to the reactions, responses, and feelings of the student.
- **Help parents to use objective terminology.** If parents use terms such as "bully" and "victim," suggest that the parents use the terms advocated by this Method or simply talk about the behaviors involved and the effect of the behaviors.

Conversation Guidelines

When engaging with parents, educators should consider these suggestions:

- **Explain the Constructive Consequences mechanism.** Understanding how the mechanism works, particularly that there is no immediate consequence for the aggressor, can help a parent understand why punitive consequences are not used and are ineffective. Further, a parent knowing that the consequence is only applied after the aggressor is given a chance to stop but doesn't may help the parent see that the consequence is not arbitrary but a direct result of their child's behavior.

- **Have the student and parents acknowledge the behavior.** Reach consensus with the student and parents on just the behavior that the student is using. For example, state that adults have observed the student frequently mocking the target. Do not allow the effect of the behavior on the target to become a point of argument.

- **Explain how the behavior is causing harm.** Once the behavior is acknowledged, explain the harm that the behavior is causing to the target. Emphasize that the aggressor may not have recognized the harm the behavior caused. If the parent or student protests that the behavior was innocuous and could not have caused harm, explain how harm cannot be judged based on behavior but is determined by how the behavior makes the target feel. Explain that harm caused by aggression can only be determined by the target.

- **Explain the need for parent support.** Educators should help parents of an aggressor understand that the process to resolve a bullying problem is essentially a process to get their child to stop directing specific behaviors at an individual. Parents should be encouraged to support the school in getting the harmful behavior to stop. This support can include enforcement of a consequence, such as a social media restriction, when the student is not in school.

Implementation

12

> **Overview:** The Method can be implemented in a variety of ways. A full implementation is the recommended approach and involves adopting all the mechanisms over a relatively short period of time. If time or resources are not available, the mechanisms can be implemented on a rolling basis using a phased implementation approach. The student and parent education mechanisms can be implemented independently of the educator mechanisms.

Full Implementation Summary

This guide was largely structured to follow a logical order for the implementation of the Method's mechanisms. A new **Language** (chapter 1) starts the cultural and perspective shift and leads into the **Education** component (chapters 2 and 3); these two mechanisms are connected; education helps make sense of the new language.

Once bullying is clearly understood, educators can move on to learning the new processes for dealing with bullying issues, specifically **Constructive Consequences** (chapter 4) and **Chain of Custody Awareness** (chapter 5). As part of the implementation of these two mechanisms, educators need to create the logistical means of securely communicating about bullying issues.

Educators prepare for target self-identification by learning the **Target Support Five-Step Framework** (chapter 6). Educators also become familiar with the school environment changes that result in the **Removal of Barriers to Reporting** (chapter 7). Once all adults in the school are ready to provide support, the school can announce the new Method to the school community through the student **Antibullying Announcement** (chapter 8) and the **Parent Communication** (described in chapter 11 and in appendix D). The distribution of the student guide for **Student Education and Empowerment** (chapter 10) can occur at the time of the student communication.

Teachers can also start using the **Classroom Strategies** (chapter 9), which will likely surface additional bullying issues. With the prior mechanisms already in place and an understanding of how to provide support to targets, educators then have all the tools they need to provide support.

Sustainment will depend upon fidelity to the Method and the training of new staff. Self-study of this guide and awareness of the logistics for Chain of Custody Awareness should be sufficient for new hires.

Full Implementation Detail

A full implementation can occur over time, but the order of delivery is important for success. Below are the recommended steps for implementation.

Step 1: Preparation

The following steps should be completed prior to the implementation:

1. Determine how the Staff Education mechanism will be implemented. Options include distribution of this guide prior to the start of a school year to enable self-study and professional development sessions.
2. Define the logistics for the Chain of Custody Awareness communication mechanism. As mentioned in chapter 5, the communication mechanism should allow for the rapid dissemination of information of who is involved in a bullying issue to relevant educators. The means of communication must be secure. It is recommended that the communication be delivered to just those adults directly involved in an issue in order to "reduce the noise" of bullying issues that might desensitize some educators to them.
3. Ready the necessary materials, including educator guides, student guides, and the parent communication.

Step 2: Education

Provide educator guides to staff for self-study, schedule professional development sessions, or use ad hoc or existing staff meetings to discuss the Method's mechanisms.

If the school uses nonteaching monitors whose only responsibility is to oversee the cafeteria, playgrounds, morning arrival, afternoon departure, or other areas in noninstructional contexts, these individuals should be included so they understand, at a minimum, the Chain of Custody Awareness mechanism. While helpful, these individuals do not need to read the full educator guide.

Step 3: Practice

During the practice step, administrators start using Constructive Consequences when dealing with bullying problems. Teachers start using Classroom Strategies to influence student behavior, identify bullying problems, and provide student support. All educators make the Chain of

Custody Awareness mechanism part of their daily routine. The Language all educators use when engaging with students and their parents also changes during this period. As educators gain experience with the mechanisms, they can gather anecdotes about the results of the Constructive Consequences and Classroom Strategies mechanisms in preparation for parent questions or a parent overview session.

Please note that practice is critical because this Method is designed to address bullying problems in a way that supports student needs, which establishes trust between students and educators. If educators are not yet practiced on the mechanisms, and bullying problems following the student rollout are not handled according to the Method's guidelines, student trust may be broken.

Step 4: Student and Parent Engagement

Deliver the first Antibullying Announcement. Explain the changes, including how Constructive Consequences and Chain of Custody Awareness work. Distribute the student guides and send the parent communication.

Consider hosting a parent forum with appropriate staff (school leadership and counseling, along with teachers who can provide insights from the practice period). Expect attendance from parents whose children are the targets of bullying behavior and passionate questions. Be prepared to explain how this Method complements existing state and district requirements and the benefits that it provides over the traditional approaches.

Post-Implementation

The first few days after the student rollout may result in a significant number of students asking for help. This is a wonderful opportunity for educators to practice providing support. Some students will eagerly try the responses that can make bullying ineffective. Others will want help from adults to get bullying to stop. How these cases are handled is critical to the Method's success.

When educators get it right by employing the Method's mechanisms, the school will be transformed. Not only will bullying problems be easier to resolve, but the overall rate of bullying incidents should drop as students use their new knowledge to prevent themselves from being bullied and to help peers who are. And over time, as students feel empowered to help peers and teachers use the Classroom Strategies to influence positive action, the level of student acceptance of aggression to positively affect social status should fall.

Administrators can also positively influence bullying levels in the school. In conversations with aggressors, the principal will develop stronger personal relationships with these students, many of whom may have influence over the level of peer acceptance of aggression. A resourceful principal will be able to foster and use these relationships to effect positive change.

Parents can also become partners in transforming the school. Parents will not just rely on the school to "fix problems" but will know actions they can take with their children to effect positive change. They will better understand the challenges educators face in resolving bullying issues. They will not put all the responsibility on the school to solve problems but will share the responsibility.

With all adults in the school community working together, students will no longer feel that they need to face bullying problems alone. They'll know that if they need help, they can reach out to any adult who will help them in the way they want to be helped.

Phased Implementation

A school interested in a less formal implementation can adopt the mechanisms over time. Administrators can start with implementing Constructive Consequences and an informal Chain of Custody Awareness, where the principal makes educators who are with the aggressor and target aware through direct conversation and/or simply rely on the target to report any further instances of aggression. Staff are educated over time as bullying issues arise; each bullying incident is used to educate those staff and the students who are directly involved. Parents are also directed to the CirclePoint website for more information as the need arises. Over time, the consistent handling of bullying issues by administration, and the education of staff, students, and parents on an as-needed basis, should result in an educated school community that applies the bullying prevention and resolution mechanisms of this Method.

Classroom Sessions to Supplement Student Self-Study

Just as not every student will pay attention to every Antibullying Announcement, not every student will read the student guide, particularly those who are not having or have not had a bullying problem. To ensure that all students get an understanding of bullying and the empowerment techniques, schools may want to conduct education sessions for students, ideally at the class level. These sessions should be interactive and cover the same material as the student guide. The school should conduct classroom sessions when the Method is implemented and annually thereafter. A sample student education session outline is provided in appendix C.

Documentation of Bullying Issues

Given the shifting legal landscape in terms of responsibility and accountability for resolution of bullying issues, administrators may wish to get a legal opinion on the advisability of documenting the efforts educators make in each bullying case. Documentation of the Constructive Consequences conversation, Chain of Custody Awareness conducted via written communications, explicit reports by educators monitoring students on whether or not the aggression has stopped, notes on the target support steps taken, and notes on parent engagement, if any, can all demonstrate that administrators took appropriate steps to address a bullying problem. In addition to liability considerations, documentation may be helpful in supporting students as they progress through their school years in terms of a record of behaviors and personal growth and development.

Appendix A: Problems with Traditional Bullying Definitions

> **Overview:** Traditional bullying definitions contain inaccuracies including the notions that aggressors intend harm; behaviors must be repeated to qualify as bullying; and bullying involves a "power imbalance." In addition, the traditional definitions focus on the aggressor and not on the target. These inaccuracies and misplaced emphasis on the aggressor lead to ineffective policies and procedures for addressing bullying issues. This appendix is intended to help a school or district understand the problems with the traditional definitions and provides the rationale for adopting the accurate definition in this guide.

Background

Western society is permeated by myths and misinformation about bullying. This misinformation includes the ideas that bullying is "mean" or "cruel" behavior intended to cause harm; that children learn bullying behavior at home or as a result of poor parenting; that punishment is an effective way to deal with bullying; that bullying occurs due to one or more "powers" that are out of balance between the aggressor and target; that some kids who are bullied are "powerless" to get the bullying to stop; that rules against bullying can work; that adults can somehow judge when bullying is occurring between students based on observed behaviors; that students who bully are "evil" or "bad characters" who go on to a life of crime, drug use, or are unable to have positive relationships; and that the solutions to driving positive behavioral change in students include putting up posters, wearing rubber bracelets, and "teaching kindness."

A primary source of these myths and misinformation about bullying is a legacy definition of bullying initially proposed by Norwegian researcher Dan Olweus in the 1960s that evolved to include the erroneous notions that bullying involves an intent to harm, involves repetition of behaviors, and is characterized by a "power imbalance" between the aggressor and target. Researchers have used this flawed definition for decades as the basis for subsequent bullying research, which in turn has led to the development and use of flawed policies.

Although some researchers recognized the flaws in this definition, the lack of widespread recognition and acceptance of those flaws meant that Olweus's ideas stood as a basis for subsequent work. Recently, however, researchers have formally acknowledged the problems with the traditional bullying definition. This awareness and a history of the evolution of the understanding of bullying can be found in the article titled "Bullying and the Abuse of Power" in *International Journal of Bullying Prevention* (ref: Andrews, et al.).

While researchers have finally come to recognize that these early ideas of Olweus are inaccurate, the definition's influence remains, meaning that educators must take it upon themselves to understand the flaws and identify and replace problematic policies based on it.

Traditional Bullying Definition Annotated

While notions of repetition, intent to harm, and power imbalances are finally starting to be rejected by researchers, they remain in current, published definitions relied on by schools, organizations, and even the US government. In addition, these definitions fail to include the understanding of bullying as a behavior driven by a need for social status. This results in definitions that use vague language and phrases that sound scientific but are obvious and redundant. Furthermore, the focus is often placed on the behavior and the aggressor, not the harm and the target. A perfect example is the following definition, taken from www.stopbullying.gov, the official bullying prevention website of the US government (accessed 10/11/2023). The superscript reference numbers have been added, with the key below the definition.

> *Bullying is unwanted, aggressive behavior[1] among school aged children that involves a real or perceived power imbalance.[2] The behavior is repeated,[3] or has the potential to be repeated,[4] over time. Both kids who are bullied and who bully others may have serious, lasting problems.[5]*
>
> *In order to be considered bullying, the behavior must be aggressive[6] and include:*
>
> - *An Imbalance of Power: Kids who bully use their power—such as physical strength,[7] access to embarrassing information, or popularity—to control or harm others.[8] Power imbalances can change over time and in different situations, even if they involve the same people.[9]*
> - *Repetition: Bullying behaviors happen more than once or have the potential to happen more than once.[10]*
>
> *Bullying includes actions such as making threats, spreading rumors, attacking someone physically or verbally, and excluding someone from a group on purpose.[11]*

While this definition has discarded the notion that students intend harm, the definition is still problematic because it is inaccurate, abstract, vague, and full of redundancies:

1. *unwanted, aggressive behavior*: Much of the aggression among school-age children is unwanted; however, it is not bullying. Only aggression that causes harm is bullying.

2. *real or perceived power imbalance*: What this phrase is trying to say is that the aggressor generally has a higher social status than the target. Physical strength is often cited as a "power" that is out of balance, but that is not true; it is the ability of the aggressor to intimidate and instill fear in a target that makes dominance aggression successful. This phrase is extremely counterproductive because it can lead adults who deal with a bullying problem to try to find and address "powers" that are out of balance. An extreme example is a school that made a list of "powers" that could be out of balance and then set a threshold for how many powers needed to be involved in instances of aggression for the aggression to qualify as bullying. The scholarship on this point has evolved, where early scholarship closest to the time of Olweus's work cites definite powers such as physical strength while later scholarship claims that powers are definitely there but may not be perceptible to adults. This is a good example of the bullying research paradox, where instead of admitting that this notion of a power imbalance is wrong, the definition implies that the notion is a fact but says the powers simply aren't apparent, i.e., it's a matter of faith.

3. *behavior is repeated*: Repetition is certainly a characteristic of some types of aggression, but not all types, and repetition is not necessary for harm to occur. Repetition is common in dominance and rejective aggression but is hard to distinguish in relational aggression. Repetition may be collective (e.g., isolated instances of rejective aggression directed at a target by an entire class). Repetition has some value in identifying bullying and is most valuable when identified as it pinpoints behavior that can be stopped or changed; however, its inclusion in definitions fails targets who are harmed by aggression for which adults cannot identify or perceive repeated aggression from the same individual.

4. *behavior . . . has the potential to be repeated*: Any single instance of just about any behavior has the potential to be repeated, but that doesn't make it bullying.

5. *both kids who are bullied and who bully others may have serious, lasting problems*: Given that almost all students at one time or another have used aggression that caused harm and/or were bullied during their school years, the link between bullying and serious lasting problems is tenuous. Bullying that is a result of a mental health issue, such as a personality disorder, that would affect a person for their entire lives is limited to a very small subset of the students who use aggression or are targets of it. If this part of the definition of bullying were accurate, then almost everyone will have or does have serious lasting problems.

6. *in order to be considered bullying, the behavior must be aggressive*: This is a fallacy based on the idea that bullying can be determined from observed behavior. What exactly does it mean to be "aggressive"? A student glancing at another can appear innocuous, but to a target of dominance aggression it can cause overwhelming fear. A student walking past another in silence can be devastating if one of them is a target of relational aggression. A whole host of behaviors involved in bullying would not fit the definition of "aggressive" to a reasonable observer. Based on this phrase alone, a significant percentage of instances of bullying would not meet the definition.

7. *kids who bully use their power—such as physical strength*: If this were true, then the solution to bullying involving dominance aggression would be to send targets to the gym to get stronger. But any reasonable person knows that's just plain silly. Silly statements do not translate into effective policy.

8. *kids who bully use their power . . . to control . . . others*: What does that even mean? A student with a higher social status can indirectly influence the behavior of the target to try to gain the approval of the aggressor. An aggressor can, for example, threaten to release embarrassing information online if the target doesn't do certain things, but that's blackmail. And a danger that this phrase actually introduces is that it can allow targets to claim that they are not responsible for their actions that were in response to bullying because, by the definition, the aggressor was using his power to control the target. A definition that absolves a student of responsibility for his actions based on the behavior of another student is dangerous.

9. *power imbalances can change over time and in different situations, even if they involve the same people*: While a student's position on the social hierarchy can change over time, and a changing social standing can enable him to be the aggressor at one point and cause him to be the target at another (or even both at the same time), how does this statement help a school administrator define policies and concrete actions for addressing bullying problems?

10. *bullying behaviors happen more than once or have the potential to happen more than once*: As noted above, this is just repetition that fluffs the definition.

11. *bullying includes actions such as making threats, spreading rumors, attacking someone physically or verbally, and excluding someone from a group on purpose*: Bullying is actually any behavior that is intended by the aggressor to have a positive effect on social status that causes harm to the target. The behaviors that can cause harm are infinite. Providing a limited list risks educators dismissing behaviors that cause harm but are not on the list.

What About the Target?

Arguably the biggest problem with definitions like those similar to the one found on stopbullying.gov is that they say <u>nothing</u> about the target and the harm suffered beyond the general statement about suffering lifelong problems and that bullying will "harm others." This problem with the definition is occasionally noted in academic works, e.g., ". . . the response of the victim is the determinant of severity and impact. A perpetrator may justify his or her actions by thinking they are trivial or humorous, but if the recipient is hurt, that is the measure of impact that matters" (ref: Bauman).

In other words, bullying is not just the behavior of the aggressor like the traditional definition implies, but occurs when aggression causes harm. Harm is what determines when aggression can be classified as bullying. And, respectfully, Professor Bauman should note that "justification" for aggressors' actions is not needed because harm is not intended. A better way to say it would be that a perpetrator [aggressor] may not realize the harm caused by his or her actions because, from the perpetrator's perspective, they appear to be trivial or humorous and are not intended to cause harm.

The critical need for educators to take action is not because students are using aggression, as implied by the behavioral focus of the stopbullying.gov definition. Instead, action is critical because of the instances of aggression that result in harm to the target. Acknowledging the harm caused to targets, however, would then require actions to help support the target by reversing the harm. It is unfortunate for students that the widely used traditional definitions of bullying barely acknowledge the harm.

The Notion of a "Power Imbalance"

The term "power imbalance" is frequently included in definitions of bullying and needs to be addressed in detail due to its pervasiveness and how this notion becomes the basis for approaches to address a bullying problem. This term is confusing because it suggests that there is a concrete characteristic, such as physical strength, that is unequal between the aggressor and target that allows the aggressor to act with impunity and prevents the target from getting the bullying to stop. This misunderstanding of what a power imbalance is can lead to unfortunate and ineffective policies and procedures, such as having a list of powers that can be "out of balance" and taking action to "restore" the balance of these powers as a solution to the bullying problem. But a power imbalance is not caused by any concrete characteristic or power of the aggressor, such as physical strength, background, popularity, ethnicity, or socioeconomic status.

What the term "power imbalance" refers to is the fact that the aggressor and the target occupy two different places in the peer group social hierarchy. This results in the higher-status aggressor being able to direct aggression at the lower-status target without fear of having peers come to the defense of the target. This difference in social status and peer support is what creates a power imbalance. A contributor to the power imbalance is that targets often haven't been taught how to respond to aggression to render it ineffective at providing a social benefit to the aggressor. Empowerment techniques can, in a sense, create a balance of power by compensating for the social hierarchy difference.

Adults actually create a power imbalance between the aggressor and target when they fail to respond to a target's request for help. An educator who decides that the aggressor's behavior is not a problem creates a feeling of powerlessness in the target. A popular student who is well-liked or favored by educators may be able to get away with harmful aggression against a target without consequence. Similarly, an educator's negative feelings toward a target may result in the educator inadvertently allowing aggression to be directed at that target. Such failures to respond to requests for help make targets feel powerless.

Adults also create power imbalances through their responses to bullying problems. Educators who punish students for bullying may actually increase the bullying. Worse, educators who investigate bullying problems and conclude that the harmed targets are not really being harmed are essentially telling targets that they won't get help from adults, which makes targets feel powerless.

The power imbalances as described above can be eliminated through social status changes, empowerment education, and changes to adult actions. A target who manages to increase his social status may no longer feel the peer rejection caused by the aggression and may be able to enlist peer support in the face of future aggression. A target who learns ways to render the aggression ineffective at providing the aggressor with a benefit to social status may get the aggression to stop. And schools that implement effective mechanisms for resolving bullying problems and providing target support immediately establish a balance of power for all students in that students are able to engage an adult for support at the first instance of harmful aggression.

Policy Problems Stemming from the Traditional Definition

The focus on the aggressor's behavior in the traditional definition results in school policies that are focused on making judgments about the behavior and leveling punitive consequences. This behavioral focus requires baselines and thresholds to be set against which the behaviors can be judged but results, unfortunately, in ineffective and counterproductive approaches to prevention and resolution. The issues with the policies based on traditional definitions are discussed in appendix B.

Appendix B: Problems with Traditional Prevention Practices

Overview: Bullying prevention programs have been around for decades. Schools have had bullying-related policies and procedures in place for decades as well. And state governments have passed laws that have codified certain policies and procedures. However, research has shown, and the experiences of educators can confirm, that these legacy programs, such as the Olweus Bullying Prevention Program, and traditional policies and procedures are generally ineffective. The reason they don't work is that they are based on traditional definitions of bullying (see appendix A), which researchers have only recently acknowledged are flawed and inaccurate. Schools and districts now have the challenge of identifying ineffective policies and procedures based on the traditional definitions and replacing them with effective mechanisms based on an accurate definition.

Problems with Common Practices

Policies and procedures based on the traditional definition of bullying are often ineffective and occasionally counterproductive. Below are seven common problems with traditional practices and the effective mechanism(s) that can be used in their place.

Problem 1: Impersonal Reporting Mechanisms

Many schools use a reporting mechanism such as an online form specifically for reporting bullying issues. These reporting mechanisms are sometimes required by district policy and are advertised to the school community. Some of these reporting mechanisms allow for anonymity and some specify that all reports will be investigated. The problem with this approach is that it creates a barrier to reporting as the mechanism runs counter to what targets need.

Bullying is a personal problem that can make a target feel ashamed or embarrassed. Targets fear that others, particularly peers, will find out about the problem, which can result in a significant social cost. Targets also fear losing control over how a bullying problem is handled. Targets are most likely to report a bullying problem if they can talk to someone they trust who they know will keep the information confidential, will not take unilateral action, and will discuss options before collaboratively deciding on a plan for resolution.

An impersonal online reporting form meets none of those needs. Targets fear that reporting via an online form will result in wider awareness of their problem. And once reported, they may lose control over how it is handled. While students are routinely counseled not to share private or embarrassing information electronically since doing so risks losing control over who sees it, online reporting forms require them to do exactly that. Since targets don't know who sees or accesses the information and how the problem will be handled, they are reluctant to report bullying problems through an online form.

Anonymity is also not a benefit. Educators need to know who is being harmed in order to provide effective support and provide targets with an opportunity to handle the problem on their own if they wish. Treating bullying reporting mechanisms like a confidential tip line to the police where an informant provides information and then lets the authorities handle it is not effective for bullying issues. Certainly this approach would seem logical to educators who treat bullying as a discipline code violation and apply punitive consequences in order to ensure no retaliation against the target. But as noted below, punishment for bullying is not just ineffective, but counterproductive. An anonymous bullying reporting mechanism is an indication that the school's approach to handling bullying problems is also flawed.

Schools have at least two solutions to the problem of the impersonal, formal reporting mechanism. First, they can implement an informal reporting mechanism in parallel with their formal reporting mechanism and let students know that they can talk confidentially to any adult in the school, the person they feel most comfortable engaging, and that adult will listen, provide suggestions for resolution, and work with the student on a plan to get the bullying to stop. In other words, if the district policy requires schools to have an online reporting form, just leave it but let students know they can also reach out to any adult they trust to talk about their problem.

Second, the school can repurpose their current informal reporting form to align with target needs by letting students know exactly who sees the information and how reports are handled, specifically that the principal first talks to the target to learn more and to develop a plan on addressing the problem. Targets will feel comfortable using the mechanism knowing that reports are confidential and that they will not lose control over how the matter is handled. This approach, however, may require an update to the policy on how bullying problems are handled to replace problematic resolution steps (e.g., punishment) with effective ones.

Problem 2: Investigations That Delay Action

Many traditional approaches involve or require an investigation by the principal to determine whether or not bullying is occurring. The investigation is stipulated because the consequence for bullying is punitive, and only the principal can determine if a student should be punished. The principal is required to take time to gather "facts" that will enable a judgment.

While the investigation is ongoing, a target and often his parents are left waiting anxiously to learn whether or not the principal will believe the target and provide a measure of relief. This wait and associated anxiety are unnecessary. The principal should take the target at his word that the aggression is causing harm and pledge to get the aggression to stop, which provides instant relief to the target.

Investigations may be required if targets are reluctant to share information out of fear of retribution or the problem becoming worse, but otherwise the principal will have all the information she needs from talking with the target to take the next step in getting the aggression to stop. Taking action without delay allows the target and parents to avoid unnecessary anxiety and the principal to save significant time in resolving the bullying problem.

Problem 3: A Judgment on Whether Bullying Is Occurring

After a principal conducts an investigation, she will then render a judgment as to whether or not bullying is occurring. The need for a judgment generally stems from the use of a traditional bullying definition that sets thresholds for bullying behavior based on the false notions of intent to harm, repetition, and/or a power imbalance, and the policy of leveling punitive consequences for bullying, which are ineffective and often counterproductive.

The principal either decides that bullying is occurring and applies a punitive consequence to the aggressor, which the aggressor views as an injustice, or the principal decides that bullying is not occurring, which essentially tells a harmed target that adults don't believe him, the aggression is approved to continue, he has no recourse through school policy, and educators will not help him. The "ruling" is always an injustice for one student and likely requires the principal to spend additional time in meetings with at least one set of unhappy parents. And the principal has made the problem worse for the target.

The solution is for the principal to listen to the target and take him at his word that the aggression is causing harm. No one can dispute that fact. And no one can dispute the aggressor's contention that he did not intend harm. A judgment becomes unnecessary because the goals are to get the aggression directed at the target to stop and to provide support to the target, neither of which is achieved through the use of punitive consequences (see problem 5, below).

Problem 4: The Focus on Behaviors Instead of the Harm

Traditional approaches to resolving bullying problems often focus on the behavior of the aggressor, as though a crime may be occurring and the principal needs to either stop the crime and punish the perpetrator or acquit the aggressor of all charges. That the focus is on the behaviors is understandable because traditional definitions of bullying try to define the problem in the context of the behavior and not in terms of the harm to the target. Administrators who are trying to determine if bullying is occurring spend their time trying to discern "power imbalances," identify repetition of behavior, and somehow deduce what is going on in the mind of the aggressor in order to judge the intent.

This focus on the behavior of the aggressor takes the attention away from the real problem, which is the harm that is being inflicted upon the target. This results in programs and policies that focus on what to do with the aggressor once found guilty of bullying but say nothing about how to help the target who has been harmed. This is akin to police hauling off the perpetrator of a violent crime but doing nothing to help the injured victim.

When the focus is flipped to the target, policies and procedures become clear. Targets need help and a way of confidentially asking for it. Targets need support to get the aggression to stop and to reverse the harm caused by the aggression. Targets also need education on bullying so they can learn ways to effectively respond to it. Targets will not reach out for help if the actions the adults take result in wider awareness of the problem, retaliation by the aggressor against the target, a social cost to the target, or risk of dismissal of the problem as not being a problem. This is the lens through which policies and procedures should be viewed and either adopted as being helpful in solving the problem (harm to target) or discarded due to being ineffective or counterproductive.

Schools seeking to resolve bullying problems should change their focus from the behavior of the aggressor to the harm being caused to the target. Starting with the target can confirm that bullying is occurring, allowing administrators to immediately stop the harmful behavior if necessary, and can provide educators with an opportunity to help targets heal and empower them with responses to aggression to render it less effective in the future. And in some instances, target empowerment enables the target to get the bullying to stop without administrators having to engage the aggressor.

Problem 5: Punishment for Bullying

Traditional approaches often use punitive consequences for bullying. The use of punitive consequences is often based on the erroneous notion of "intent to harm" and that aggressive behavior may *appear* to be mean and cruel to an observer. But because punishment as a solution to bullying is based on a flawed understanding of the problem, punishment as a solution is likewise flawed and ineffective and often makes the problem worse.

Punishment as a consequence for bullying is ineffective for the following reasons:

- Since aggressors are not using aggression to intentionally harm targets, a punitive consequence is viewed by the aggressor (and his parents) as unfair and unjust. An aggressor may legitimately (from his perspective) claim innocence, convince his parents of this fact, and enlist their support against the school's administration.
- An aggressor who directs identical aggression at multiple individuals, including friends, or sees peers engaging in identical behaviors, views punishment as inconsistent and unreasonable.
- Punishment that is based on the word of the target makes the target responsible for the punishment and can result in retaliation by the aggressor and peers against the target.
- In a peer group with a high level of acceptance of aggression and where the target has been chronically bullied and aggression has been normalized, peers view the aggressor's punishment as unjust and blame the target, causing a further reduction in status of the target and reinforcing any belief by the peers that the target deserves the aggression.
- Punishment can raise awareness of the bullying problem among the peer group, something the target wants to avoid since greater awareness can further reduce social status.
- Punishment of the aggressor can actually boost his social status, which provides an incentive to continue the aggression.
- Punishment serves as a very strong deterrent to reporting bullying problems because students know that reporting on a peer who then gets punished will result in retaliation or a social cost.

When punitive consequences are used to address bullying problems, no one in the process—aggressors, targets, parents, or educators—is satisfied with the result. Aggressors consider punishment an injustice. Targets, who have lost social status from bullying, experience an even greater reduction in status from getting a peer in trouble. Targets frequently suffer increased bullying when the aggressor and his friends retaliate for the punishment. Parents of the aggressor generally defend their children and view the punishment as an injustice. Parents of the target, who may feel initial relief for getting a measure of justice for their child, become frustrated that the bullying doesn't stop or gets worse for their child. And educators are left to deal with a more complicated problem that is harder and more time-consuming to solve. In short, punitive consequences serve the needs of no one and make the problem worse for everyone.

The solution is to replace punitive consequences with constructive consequences, where the aggressor is given an opportunity to avoid any consequence if the behavior stops but gets a consequence that results in a loss of social status among peers if the behavior continues. Leveraging the driver of aggression to get it to stop is an effective approach that is satisfactory to everyone involved in the process.

Problem 6: Lack of Target Support

The misguided behavioral focus of traditional policies leads to the problem of schools believing that a bullying issue has been resolved once the aggressor's behavior has been stopped. Stopping the aggressor's behavior, however, is just one step in resolving the problem. What traditional approaches neglect is helping the student harmed by the aggression.

Schools must provide support to targets to help them recover from the harm caused by bullying and by empowering them through education so that they can avoid harm in the future. Unlike wounds caused by physical harm, the wounds caused by bullying do not necessarily heal on their own over time. Intervention is sometimes required to help students through the healing process. Schools should implement a target support framework to help reverse the harm caused by bullying and to educate and empower targets to avoid harm in the future.

Problem 7: Solutions Based on the Erroneous Notion of the Intent to Harm

One problem stemming from a traditional definition of bullying is that schools mistakenly believe that they can prevent and reduce bullying through actions that focus on kindness and empathy. Schools might try to teach students to be kinder or more empathetic and to raise awareness of the harm that bullying causes by holding school assemblies, having students hang antibullying posters, passing out bullying awareness bracelets, and inviting students to take antibullying pledges.

These solutions are simply not effective. The feasibility of being able to teach students kindness and empathy notwithstanding, aggression is not driven by a lack of kindness or empathy. Aggression is driven by a need for social status, and the effect of the behavior on the target is generally not a consideration of the aggressor. The aggressor is focused on the personal benefit the behavior provides. Aggressors may change behavior when they are made aware that their behavior is causing harm. However, some aggressors will continue to use aggression even after being told that it is causing harm. Lessons on kindness and empathy will have no effect.

Another reason why teaching kindness and empathy are ineffective is that students do not always make the connection between bullying as a concept and their own behavior. Since students are not intending harm when they use aggression that results in bullying, they don't connect a lesson on being kind or how the other person feels to their own actions. Further, aggression directed at a target by a peer group becomes normalized over time such that the group won't recognize their own or their peers' behaviors as bullying. Lessons on kindness and empathy are certainly beneficial in the context of social emotional learning and personal growth; however, they are not solutions to the problem of bullying. This inability of students to make the connection between bullying as a concept and their own behavior is also why rules against bullying are ineffective.

The solution is for schools to use the same driver of aggression—to positively affect social status—to get it to stop. Students use aggression to get a social benefit; students will stop aggression in order to avoid a social cost. Depriving the aggressor of the peer audience that provides the boost in status and temporarily severing the connection to peers, which is needed to sustain social status, will motivate the aggressor to stop.

Problem 8: False Sense of Security from Published Policies

Some districts and states require schools to publish their bullying policies. The idea is that schools are demonstrating that they have a formal policy and thus the problem is under control. Publishing the policy also conveys that the school is transparent about how they handle bullying problems. A published policy implies fairness and equity in how bullying issues are handled.

Unless a school has discarded traditional policies and adopted effective mechanisms, however, the published policy is simply advertising that the school is using outdated and ineffective methods to address the problem. Publishing such policies also serves as a barrier to student reporting as students know that traditional policies are ineffective. A published policy gives educators (and elected representatives) a false sense of security that bullying issues are handled effectively and that the larger school community is confident in educators to effectively address the problem.

If schools are required to publish policies, they should ensure that they are effective. Policies based on traditional definitions need to be discarded and replaced by ones based on an accurate definition. And to give the larger school community even greater confidence in the effectiveness of these policies, educators should help educate parents on bullying to dispel myths and misunderstanding so that the rationale behind the policies is clear.

The Need for Change

The problems with traditional policies may be why bullying issues are sometimes ignored in schools. Published policy or state law requires principals to launch investigations that they know are going to make the problem worse. These policies thrust principals into the middle of he-said/she-said arguments and angry parents, trying to reach an "impartial" judgment that satisfies no one. Problematic policies that make the problem worse is what causes students to take drastic actions that can lead to tragedy, and parents to take legal action that can be extremely costly.

The unfortunate fact is that policies and laws based on traditional approaches do not provide a means for educators to effectively resolve bullying problems. These policies and laws tie their hands. Schools must adopt effective mechanisms even in environments where ineffective policies are mandated in order to provide the support and healing that targets of bullying require, to avoid tragic outcomes, and to minimize the risk of liability.

Appendix C:
Student Session Outline

> **Overview:** The following script can be used to guide a student education session. For these sessions, an educator goes to each classroom in grades 3 and up to talk about bullying, share the "bullying secrets" that every student should know about why kids bully and how to get it to stop, and tell students how adults will start handling bullying problems—the way students want them to be handled.

Please note that classroom-level sessions have been found to be the most productive due to the interactive nature of the sessions. Schools should avoid conducting a single session, i.e., an assembly-type presentation, as student questions and concerns may vary by classroom and grade. A smaller group size also allows for a much more involved discussion.

Session Outline

The student session should cover four main topics:

1. what bullying is
2. why kids do it
3. what kids can do about it
   a. as a target
   b. as a bystander
4. how adults are now going to help

Schools are welcome to develop their own session outlines. However, the following outline has been found to be extremely effective and allows an educator to complete an interactive session with a group of up to 25 students within 30–40 minutes.

Note: The text in italics are examples of what the educator leading the session can say to students and are provided to establish the context of the script outline. The educator can modify the language used and level of detail based on the grade level of the students.

Introduction

Today we are going to talk about bullying. We're going to talk about what it is, why kids do it, what you can do about it, and how adults in the school are going to start supporting you and help you with bullying problems.

Topic 1: What is bullying?

Question/discussion: *Who can tell me what bullying is? What behavior is considered bullying and what is not bullying?* Talk about bullying—what it is and what it isn't.

Key points:

- four types of bullying based on the behaviors used:
  1. physical aggression: pushing, shoving, intimidation, verbal threats
  2. verbal aggression: mocking, teasing, insulting, antagonizing
  3. written aggression: can be used to mock, tease, insult, and antagonize; can also be used to harm friendships; writing can be on physical objects or on social media
  4. friendship harming: gossip, rumors, actions intended to get others to exclude a person or not want to be friends with a person
- cyberbullying is not a type of bullying. It is just the use of social media to direct aggression at others.
- bullying is NOT just the behavior/aggression:
  ◦ bullying = aggression + <u>emotional harm</u>;
  ◦ emotional harm is more than just "being bothered." It is feeling scared, feeling sick, not wanting to come to school, feeling flawed, feeling like there is something wrong with you, feeling that classmates don't like you, feeling like you don't belong, and/or feeling isolated and alone.
- appropriate terms:
  ◦ aggressor: person who is using the bullying behavior. This person is not called a "bully."
  ◦ target: person who is harmed by the bullying behavior. This person is not called a "victim."

Topic 2: Why do kids bully others? The secrets of bullying behavior

Question/discussion: *Why do kids use bullying behaviors? Why do kids tease others, make fun of others, push each other around, exclude others, and stop being friends with someone because another person asks them to?* Emphasize that bullying behaviors do not always result in bullying. They are just a type of social interaction.

Key points:

- The aggression used in bullying is generally NOT intended to cause harm.
- While it may *seem* that an aggressor is trying to cause harm, the aggressor is really just trying to make herself more popular. The aggressor may also feel threatened by the target in terms of the target somehow causing the aggressor to be less popular. While getting a target upset can make the aggression even more effective at making the aggressor popular, it is not necessary and not the goal.
- Bullying secret 1: physical aggression is intended to make a target show fear so that others watching will think the aggressor is someone to be afraid of and will give the aggressor respect. If the target does not show fear, even if the target feels fear, the aggressor does not get respect from others, and the aggression should stop. If the target is not intimidated or does not feel fear, bullying does not occur.
- Bullying secret 2: verbal aggression and some written aggression are intended to make the aggressor appear clever to others and entertain others watching to gain their admiration. The aggressor can entertain others no matter how the target reacts. If the target gets visibly upset, the behavior can be more entertaining. If the target's feelings are not hurt by what is said, bullying does not occur.
- Bullying secret 3: friendship harming, which can include some written aggression, is intended to help the aggressor protect her own popularity. The aggressor feels that the target threatens her popularity, so she rallies others to her side and has them take a stand against the target. The aggressor feels reassured when everyone takes her side. In cases where an aggressor uses friendship harming to get back at someone for an offense, the purpose of the bullying is to get justice by hurting the offender. Once the offender loses friends and has a reduced social status, the aggressor feels satisfied. But if the aggressor does not rally others to her side or others do not participate in the aggression, bullying does not occur.

Topic 3: What can you do about bullying that is affecting you, a friend, or another student?

Question/discussion: *Now that you know the bullying secrets and how bullying behaviors work, what can you do about bullying? What can you do if you are being bullied? What can you do if a friend or a classmate is being bullied?* Note that the educator leading the student session should review and understand the target and bystander empowerment sections of chapter 10.

- **Physical aggression** is effective and is repeated if the target shows fear. The way to counteract physical aggression is not to show fear. Know that the intent of physical bullying is not harm but to make the person afraid in front of others. A target who shows no fear makes the aggression fail in providing the aggressor with respect from those watching.

- **Verbal and written aggression** can be effective no matter how the target responds but is certain to be repeated if the target gets visibly upset or responds with similar verbal or written aggression. A target should try not to get visibly upset or use the same aggression in response. Targets should appear unaffected, laugh along with the aggressor, agree with the aggressor, or do something funny and unexpected. Know that if a characteristic is being used—if the aggressor is making fun of or mocking some aspect of the target—the characteristic is not a flaw, just a way to try to get others to laugh or a way to get the target upset.
- **Friendship harming** is guaranteed to be successful if the target pretends it is not happening and/or hopes it will pass. A target must take action! The target should find out who the aggressor is and why she is doing it. The target should talk to her, or if she is not a friend, talk to a friend who may be participating in the bullying. A target should get friends to stand with her and ask these friends to get the other participants to stop. The target should not, however, retaliate with a bullying campaign of her own.

If you see a friend or classmate being bullied and you want to get it to stop, you can do the following:

- intervene directly by taking the side of the target against the aggressor; however, this action carries risk that the aggressor and his supporters will turn against you. Direct intervention is a personal choice. Never intervene directly because an adult asks you to.
- intervene indirectly by taking the following actions:
  - interrupt the aggression as it is happening but pretend not to know it is happening
  - talk to the aggressor in private to ask him to stop
  - talk to the target in private to show you support him
  - do not agree to stop being friends with someone or to ignore someone if a person asks you to
  - be a friend to the target! Say hello when you see her. Let her know that she has friends. Merely acknowledging a fellow student can make a difference.

Topic 4: How adults are now going to help

This part of the discussion should be divided into two parts. The first part is to let students say why they don't ask adults for help with a bullying problem. They will likely provide this information enthusiastically or possibly in an accusatory way. They will relish the opportunity to tell adults how and why adults get it wrong. Their degree of passion in answering this question will actually reflect their perception of the degree of change that is needed to provide them with adequate support. But the question is a "set up" of sorts because the educator facilitating the session then responds to every point the students make with how the Method addresses these concerns and provides help in the way the students want to be helped.

Part 1: Why don't kids ask for adult help with a bullying problem?

Question/discussion: *You all know that adults do not like bullying and want to help. But why don't kids tell adults when they are being bullied or ask for help?* Students will provide some or all of the following answers or even some new ones:

- Adults punish aggressors, which results in increased bullying due to retaliation.
- Students who tell an adult about a bullying problem may become targets themselves.
- Telling on a peer who is then punished carries a negative social cost; getting a peer in trouble is "not cool," and the student who told may be ostracized by peers.
- A target doesn't want others to know about the problem; however, adults frequently make a big deal out of it, which makes peers aware.
- Once a target tells an adult, the target loses control over how the problem is handled; the target may just want to talk to an adult and get advice, not have the adult take action.
- A target doesn't want an aggressor to know that the bullying behavior is effective; however, the way adults confront the aggressor, by linking the punishment to the harm, does exactly that.
- The reliance by adults on target or bystander reports in confronting the aggressor, and the aggressor's desire to avoid punishment, often result in a he-said/she-said impasse where adults have no idea who is telling the truth and thus take no action.
- Bullying frequently occurs out of sight of adults; simply making one adult aware means that the problem migrates to times and places where that adult is not present or goes online.
- Schools often require reporting of this highly personal and, to targets, sometimes embarrassing problem—one that targets at most only want to reveal to a very trusted individual—by filling out a form and then handing it to some administrator in the office for "processing," where, for all the target knows, it could be left out for anyone to see.
- Adults are sometimes dismissive when students try to report a problem, or they give ineffective responses such as telling students just to ignore the aggressor.
- Bullying can take place through social media, and adults don't understand the technology.

Part 2: How adults will help going forward

Question/discussion: *You are right. All those things you said about why students don't go to an adult for help with bullying are a problem. But adults in this school want to fix that problem. So we've made some changes about how we are going to handle bullying problems. Here is what we will be doing now:*

- *We will no longer punish aggressors. Instead, we will give aggressors a chance to change their behavior and stop their aggression and avoid a consequence.*

- *We will not use the names of anyone who reports a bullying problem in the conversation with the aggressor. If you report a bullying problem, we will try to observe it first so we can see it for ourselves, and the conversation with the aggressor will be about what we have witnessed and not what anyone has reported. We will not reveal who reported a bullying problem.*

- *Since there is no longer immediate punishment for bullying, a person who reports a bullying problem will not get a peer in trouble. The only time a person will have a consequence for bullying is if he continues the bullying behavior after we ask that person to stop.*

- *We will not make a big deal out of bullying problems. We will handle bullying problems quietly and confidentially. Only those who need to know to get the problem to stop will know.*

- *If you want to talk about a bullying problem, you can ask any adult for help. And when you talk to an adult about a bullying problem, it does not mean the adult is going to run off and do something. You can ask an adult for help just to get advice. You don't even need to provide the names of anyone who is bullying you. And if you do want the adult to help solve the problem, you and the adult will determine a course of action together. You will have a say in how the problem is addressed.*

- *When we talk to an aggressor who is bullying someone, we will talk about the behavior that we see, not about the hurt the aggressor is causing. The discussion will be all about changing behavior.*

- *When we ask an aggressor to change behavior, we will also notify all the adults—teachers, specialists, monitors, etc.—who are with the aggressor and the target during the day about the problem so they can keep watch and ensure that the bullying behavior stops. Aggressors will no longer be able to bully when adults are not watching. Adults will be watching, and the aggressor will know that.*

- *We will make it clear to aggressors that the bullying should not continue via social media. We will ask targets to show us if bullying continues over social media after we've asked the aggressor to stop. If bullying continues over social media, the aggressor will be prevented from using social media at school. In addition, we will contact the aggressor's parents to ensure the bullying does not continue after school.*

- *We will take all reports of bullying seriously. We will not dismiss any requests for help.*

- *We are all here to help you. If you want help with a bullying problem, you can ask any adult in the school for help. All requests for help will be private and confidential.*

Starting today, this is what we are committing to you. We are going to do our best to help you the way you want to be helped. And if we don't get it right the first time, we want you to tell us that so we can get it right the next time. Our goal with this new way of addressing bullying problems is to help the right way.

And for those of you who want to solve a bullying problem on your own, whether you are bullied or someone you know is being bullied, we have a guide for you that talks about ways you can get bullying to stop on your own. But know, however, that if you try yourself and you can't get the bullying to stop, we'll still be here to help you.

Appendix D:
Sample Parent Communication

The following sample letter can be used as a model for a communication to parents about the adoption of the CirclePoint Method:

Dear Parents and Caregivers:

Our school is implementing a new bullying prevention method, called CirclePoint. This research-based method involves the entire school community and provides all members—administrators, teachers, specialists, nonteaching staff, parents, and students—with effective role-appropriate actions, strategies, and processes for preventing and stopping bullying.

The method's mechanisms for addressing bullying are designed to get bullying issues to resolve without punitive consequences. In addition, the heightened monitoring mechanism enables adults to monitor the students involved in known bullying problems, which will help those affected to feel safer. The method also enables us to provide support to affected students and to use proactive and reactive bullying prevention strategies in the classroom.

We actually began slowly introducing the staff-based components of the method over the past [INSET TIME FRAME] and we are pleased to report [INSERT ADMINISTRATION'S VIEWS ON THE METHOD'S EFFECTIVENESS].

We are very excited to implement the final components of the method, specifically student and parent awareness and education. Students in grades 3–8 will receive a bullying prevention guide that teaches about bullying and how to respond to aggression to render it ineffective. The CirclePoint website (www.circlepointbullying.com) provides information for parents on bullying and support strategies. The website also has detailed information about the new method. We strongly encourage you to review this information.

We are pleased with the results of the method thus far and we're excited to fully complete the implementation. The method promises to not just allow us to more easily prevent bullying and resolve incidents when they occur but holds the promise of transforming our school to make bullying among students less socially acceptable. Please let us know if you have any questions about the method, or visit the CirclePoint website for more information.

Acknowledgments

A huge thanks to Michele Davis, Principal of the Warren Prescott K–8 School, Boston Public Schools, and Dr. Domenic Amara, former Academic Superintendent for Middle and K–8 Schools, Boston Public Schools, for providing the impetus to create the CirclePoint Program from which this Method was derived and for their input, feedback, and support during the program development; Karen Elias, Kindergarten Teacher and Teacher in Charge, Boston Public Schools, for her invaluable feedback and insights; and the teachers, parents, and students of the Warren Prescott K–8 School in Charlestown, Massachusetts, for their support in piloting the CirclePoint Program.

Thanks also to Israel C. Kalman, MS, a noted school psychologist, psychotherapist, lecturer, author, bullying expert, and reviewer and critic of bullying prevention programs, for his support and invaluable guidance on various bullying concepts. Many of the individual empowerment techniques in this guide are based on those contained in his books *Bullies to Buddies: How to Turn Your Enemies into Friends* and *Super-Dren the De-Victimizer*.

And a special thanks to Susan Hayward, principal of the Holden Christian Academy in Holden, Massachusetts, for her feedback on an early version of this guide.

About the Author

Ari Magnusson worked for seven years as the bullying prevention educator for the Massachusetts General Hospital's Life Skills program offered in Boston, Massachusetts-area schools in the United States. At the request of Boston Public Schools, he created the CirclePoint Bullying Prevention Program, which was piloted to great success. For the past decade, he has been teaching about bullying at the elementary, middle, and high school levels in person and virtually. He has worked with educators on implementing whole-school solutions and has helped educators, parents, and students resolve individual bullying problems. He has also provided guidance to healthcare practitioners on how to support their patients and their caregivers when they identify a bullying issue.

Sources

Andrews, Naomi C. Z., et al. "Bullying and the Abuse of Power." *International Journal of Bullying Prevention* (2023). https://doi.org/10.1007/s42380-023-00170-0

Anthony, Michelle, and Reyna Lindert. *Little Girls Can Be Mean: Four Steps to Bully-Proof Girls in the Early Grades.* New York: St. Martin's Press, 2010.

Atlas, Rona S., and Debra J. Pepler. "Observations of bullying in the classroom." *Journal of Educational Research* 92 (1998): 86–99.

Bakken, Linda, Neilia Solberg, and Chris Gentess. "Middle School Cyberbullying Curriculum." Seattle Public Schools, fall 2008. http://district.seattleschools.org/modules/cms/pages.phtml?pageid=216981

Bauer, Nerissa S., Paula Lozano, and Frederick P. Rivara. "The Effectiveness of the Olweus Bullying Prevention Program in Public Middle Schools: A Controlled Trial," *Journal of Adolescent Health*, March 2007, vol. 40, issue 3, pp. 266–274.

Bauman, Sheri. *Cyberbullying: What Counselors Need to Know.* Alexandria: American Counseling Association, 2011.

Black, Sally D. "Evaluation of the Olweus Bullying Prevention Program: How the Program Can Work for Inner City Youth" (a report from the *Proceedings of Persistently Safe Schools: The 2007 National Conference on Safe Schools*), 2007.

Boehm, Christopher. *Hierarchy in the Forest: The Evolution of Egalitarian Behavior.* Cambridge: Harvard University Press, 1999.

Boehm, Christopher. *Moral Origins: The Evolution of Virtue, Altruism, and Shame.* New York: Basic Books, 2012.

Bonanno, Rina A., and Shelley Hymel. "Beyond Hurt Feelings: Investigating Why Some Victims of Bullying Are at Greater Risk for Suicidal Ideation." *Merrill-Palmer Quarterly* 56, Number 3 (July 2010): 420–440.

Coleman, Peter T. "Dismantling Systems of Bullying." International Center for Cooperation & Conflict Resolution, November 18, 2011. http://blogs.tc.columbia.edu/icccr/2011/11/18/dismantling-systems-of-bullying/

Coloroso, Barbara. *The Bully, the Bullied, and the Bystander.* New York: Harper, 2008.

Colvin, Geoff, et. al. "The School Bully: Assessing the Problem, Developing Interventions, and Future Research Directions." *Journal of Behavioral Education* 8:3 (1998): 293–319.

Cox, Deborah L., Sally D. Stabb, and Joseph F. Hulgus. "Anger and Depression in Girls and Boys: A Study of Gender Differences," *Psychology of Women Quarterly*, March 2000, vol. 24, no. 1, pp. 110–112.

Davis, Stan. *Schools Where Everyone Belongs: Practical Strategies for Reducing Bullying.* Illinois: Research Press, 2007.

Davis, Stan, and Charisse Nixon. "The Youth Voice Project" (the first report from the *Youth Voice Research Project*), 2010. http://www.youthvoiceproject.com

Davis, Stan, and Charisse Nixon. "The Youth Voice Project" (the second report from the *Youth Voice Research Project*), 2010. http://www.youthvoiceproject.com

Davis, Stan, and Charisse Nixon. "Youth Voice Project First Results Workshop" (a presentation to the 2010 International Bullying Prevention Association conference in Seattle, WA), 2010. http://www.youthvoiceproject.com

Dijkstra, Jan Kornelis, Siegwart Lindenberg, and Rene Veenstra. "Beyond the class norm: Bullying behavior of popular adolescents and its relation to peer acceptance and rejection." *Journal of Abnormal Child Psychology* 36 (2008): 1289–1299.

Dodge, Kenneth A., Thomas J. Dishion, and Jennifer E. Lansford. "Deviant Peer Influences in Intervention and Public Policy for Youth." *Social Policy Report* 20 (1) (2006). http://files.eric.ed.gov/fulltext/ED521749.pdf

Dowdy, June P., ed. "Bullying Prevention: A Statewide Collaborative That Works" (a report to stakeholders from PA CARES, HALT!, and the Highmark Healthy High 5 Bullying Prevention Institute), 2009.

Eliot, Megan, Dewey Cornell, Anne Gregory, and Xitao Fan. "Supportive school climate and student willingness to seek help for bullying and threats of violence." *Journal of School Psychology* 48 (2010): 533–553.

Feinberg, Ted. "Bullying Prevention and Intervention," *Principal Leadership Magazine*, vol. 4, no. 1, September 2003. http://www.nasponline.org/resources/principals/nassp_bullying.aspx

Green, Jennifer, et. al. "Identifying Bully Victims: Definitional Versus Behavioral Approaches." *Psychological Assessment* 25 (2) (2013): 651–657.

Gregory, Anne, Dewey Cornell, Xitao Fan, Peter Sheras, Tse-Hua Shih, and Franci Huang. "Authoritative school discipline: High school practices associated with lower bullying and victimization." *Journal of Educational Psychology*, 102(2), (May 2010): 483–496.

Goldman, Linda. *Raising Our Children to Be Resilient: A Guide to Helping Children Cope with Trauma in Today's World.* New York: Brunner-Routledge, 2005.

Hawkins, D. Lynn, Debra J. Pepler, and Wendy M. Craig. "Naturalistic observations of peer interventions in bullying." *Social Development* 10 (2001): 512–527.

Hinduja, Sameer, and Justin W. Patchin. *Cyberbullying: Identification, Prevention, & Response.* Cyberbullying Research Center (cyberbullying.org), 2021, accessed 10/17/2023.

Hodges, Ernest V. E., and David G. Perry. "Personal and interpersonal antecedents and consequences of victimization by peers." *Journal of Personality and Social Psychology* 76 (1999): 677–685.

Holt, Melissa K., and Melissa A. Keys. "Teachers' Attitudes toward Bullying." In Espelage, Dorothy L., and Susan M. Swearer (Eds). *Bullying in American Schools: A Social-Ecological Perspective on Prevention*. Mahwah, New Jersey: Lawrence Erlbaum Associates, Inc.: 2004: 121–122.

James, Alana. "Research Briefing: School Bullying." National Society for the Prevention of Cruelty to Children, February 2010. http://www.nspcc.org.uk/Inform/research/Briefings/school_bullying _pdf_wdf73502.pdf

Jones, Lisa, Mia Doces, Susan Swearer, and Anne Collier. "Implementing Bullying Prevention Programs in Schools: A How-To Guide" (a draft report from the Born This Way Foundation and the Berkman Center for Internet & Society at Harvard University), April 16, 2012.

Juvonen, Jaana, and Adriana Galvan. "Peer influence in involuntary social groups: Lessons from research on bullying." In Prinstein, M. and K. Dodge (Eds.). *Peer Influence Processes among Youth*. New York: Guilford Press, 2008. pp. 225–244.

Juvonen, Jaana, and Alice Y. Ho. "Social motives underlying disruptive behavior across middle grades." *Journal of Youth and Adolescence* 37 (2008): 747–756.

Juvonen, Jaana, and Sandra Graham. "Bullying in Schools: The Power of Bullies and the Plight of Victims." *Annual Review of Psychology,* 2014.65:159–185. Downloaded from www.annualreviews.org. Access provided by 173.48.111.215 on 09/22/23.

Kalman, Izzy, Lola Kalman, and Chari Pere. *Super-Dren, the De-Victimizer*. New York: The Wisdom Pages, 2010.

Kalman, Izzy. *Bullies to Buddies: How to turn your enemies into friends*. New York: The Wisdom Pages, 2010.

Kalman, Izzy. Called-out comment in "Bully Psychology: Where Evolution and Morality Collide," by Alice G. Walton. *Forbes*, July 5, 2012. http://www.forbes.com/sites/alicegwalton/2012/07/05/ bully-psychology-why-bullying-is-one-of-evolutions-big-snafus/

Kalman, Izzy. "The Anti-Bullying Operation was a Success but the Patient Died," from the blog "A Psychological Solution to Bullying" in *Psychology Today*, April 8, 2009. http://www.psychologytoday.com/blog/the-bully-witch-hunt/200904/the-anti-bully- operation-was-success -the-patient-died

Kalman, Izzy. "Ladakh: A Society with No Bullies—Or Victims!" from the blog "A Psychological Solution to Bullying" in *Psychology Today*, November 17, 2009. http://www.psychologytoday.com/blog/ psychological-solution-bullying/200911/ladakh-society-no-bullies-or-victims

Kert, Allison S., et. al. "Impact of the Word 'Bully' on the Reported Rate of Bullying Behavior." *Psychology in the Schools* 47(2) (2010).

Ladd, Gary W., and Wendy Troop-Gordon. "The role of chronic peer difficulties in the development of children's psychological adjustment problems." *Child Development* 74 (2003): 1344–1367.

Lafontana, Kathryn M., and Antonius H. N. Cillessen. "Developmental changes in the priority of perceived status in childhood and adolescence." *Social Development* 19-1 (2010): 130–147.

Larkin, Ralph W. *Comprehending Columbine*. Philadelphia: Temple University Press, 2007.

Larkin, Ralph W. "Legitimated Adolescent Violence: Lessons from Columbine." *School Shootings: International Research, Case Studies, and Concepts for Prevention*. Ed. Nils Bockler. New York: Springer, 2013, 159–176.

Lee, Talisha, and Dewey Cornell. "Concurrent Validity of the Olweus Bully/Victim Questionnaire." *Journal of School Violence* 9:1 (2009): 56–73.

Milsom, Amy, and Laura L. Gallo. "Bullying in Middle Schools: Prevention and Intervention." *Middle School Journal* 37 (3) (Jan. 2006): 12–19.

National Association of School Psychologists. "Bullying prevention and intervention in schools" [Position statement]. Bethesda, MD: Author, 2012.

Olweus, Dan. *Bullying at School: What We Know and What We Can Do*. Malden, MA: Blackwell Publishing, 1993.

Olweus, Dan. "Understanding and Researching Bullying: Some Critical Issues." In *Handbook of Bullying in Schools: An International Perspective*, edited by Shane R. Jimerson, Susan M. Swearer, Dorothy L. Espelage. New York: Routledge, 2010.

"Olweus Bullying Prevention Program," Hazelden Publishing, accessed June 4, 2012. http://www .violencepreventionworks.org/public/olweus_bullying_prevention_program.page

Olweus, Dan, and Susan P. Limber. "The Olweus Bullying Prevention Program: Implementation and Evaluation over Two Decades" (undated article to appear in *The International Handbook of School Bullying* published by Routledge, New York).

Rigby, Ph.D., Ken, and Phillip Slee, Ph.D, "Suicidal Ideation among Adolescent School Children, Involvement in Bully—Victim Problems, and Perceived Social Support." *Suicide and Life-Threatening Behavior* 29, Issue 2 (Summer 1999): 119–130.

Robison, Kathy. "Bullies and Victims: A Primer for Parents" (a report from the National Association of School Psychologists), 2010. http://www.nasponline.org/resources/bullying/index.aspx

Rossen, Eric, & Cowan, Katherine C. "A framework for school-wide bullying prevention and safety" [Brief]. Bethesda, MD: National Association of School Psychologists, 2012.

Salmivalli, Christina. "Bullying and the Peer Group: A Review." *Aggression and Violent Behavior* 15 (2010): 112–120.

Salmivalli, Christina, Arja Huttunen, and Kirsti M. J. Lagerspetz. "Peer networks and bullying in schools." *Scandinavian Journal of Psychology* 38 (1997): 305–312.

Saufler, Chuck and Cyndi Gagne. *Maine Project Against Bullying. Final Report*. Augusta: Maine State Dept. of Education, 2000.

Sawyer, Anne L., et. al. "Examining Ethnic, Gender, and Developmental Differences in the Way Children Report Being a Victim of 'Bullying' on Self-Report Measures." *Journal of Adolescent Health*, 43 (2008): 106–114.

Schmidt, John J. *Counseling in Schools: Essential Services and Comprehensive Programs*. Boston: Allyn and Bacon, 1993.

Schmidt, John J. *The Elementary/Middle School Counselor's Survival Guide, 3rd Edition*. San Francisco: Jossey-Bass, 2010.

Schuster, Beate. "Outsiders at school: The prevalence of bullying and its relation with social status." *Group Processes & Intergroup Relations* 2 (1999): 175–190.

Shelley, Louise I. "American Crime: An International Anomaly?" *Comparative Social Research* 8 (1985): 81–95.

Simmons, Rachel. *Odd Girl Out: The Hidden Culture of Aggression in Girls.* New York: Mariner Books, 2011.

Sklare, Gerald B. *Brief Counseling That Works: A Solution-Focused Approach for School Counselors and Administrators, 2nd Edition.* Thousand Oaks: Corwin Press, 2005.

Smith, Peter K. "Bullying: Recent Developments," *Child and Adolescent Mental Health*, vol. 9, no. 3, 2004, pp. 98–103.

Ttofi, Maria M., and David P. Farrington, "Effectiveness of school-based programs to reduce bullying: a systematic and meta-analytic review," *Journal of Experimental Criminology* 7 (1) (March 2011): 27–56.

Walton, Alice G. "Bully Psychology: Where Evolution and Morality Collide," *Forbes*, July 5, 2012. http://www.forbes.com/sites/alicegwalton/2012/07/05/bully-psychology-why-bullying-is-one-of-evolutions-big-snafus/

Whitted, Kathryn S., and David R. Dupper. "Best Practices for Preventing or Reducing Bullying in Schools." *Children & Schools* 27 (3) (2005): 167–175.

Wiseman, Rosalind. *Queen Bees & Wannabes: Helping Your Daughter Survive the Cliques, Gossip, Boyfriends, and the New Realities of Girl World.* New York: Three Rivers Press, 2009.

Zarate-Garza, Pablo Patricio MD, et. al. "How Well Do We Understand the Long-Term Health Implications of Childhood Bullying?" *Harvard Review of Psychiatry*, March/April 2017 25 (2): 89–95.